T0295850

Volume 6

MARKETING MANAGEMENT IN AIR TRANSPORT

MARKETING MANAGEMENT IN AIR TRANSPORT

JACK L. GRUMBRIDGE

Routledge
Taylor & Francis Group

LONDON AND NEW YORK

First published in 1966

This edition first published in 2015
by Routledge
2 Park Square, Milton Park, Abingdon, Oxon, OX14 4RN

and by Routledge
711 Third Avenue, New York, NY 10017

Routledge is an imprint of the Taylor & Francis Group, an informa business

British Library Cataloguing in Publication Data
A catalogue record for this book is available from the British Library

ISBN: 978-0-415-83446-9 (Set)
ISBN: 978-1-138-78724-7 (Volume 6)

Publisher's Note
The publisher has gone to great lengths to ensure the quality of this reprint but
points out that some imperfections in the original copies may be apparent.

Disclaimer
The publisher has made every effort to trace copyright holders and would
welcome correspondence from those they have been unable to trace.

MARKETING MANAGEMENT IN AIR TRANSPORT

Jack L. Grumbridge

London

GEORGE ALLEN & UNWIN LTD

RUSKIN HOUSE   MUSEUM STREET

FIRST PUBLISHED IN 1966

PRINTED IN GREAT BRITAIN
in 10 on 11 point Times Roman type
BY UNWIN BROTHERS LTD
WOKING AND LONDON

This book is dedicated to
HENRY J. A. HILL, M.B.E.
as a personal tribute to the
distinction he has brought to
British airline salesmanship

ACKNOWLEDGMENTS

In writing this book I have called unashamedly on several of my colleagues and friends to check over draft chapters dealing with subjects of which they have particular expert knowledge. My thanks in this connection are specially due to Messrs Gilbert, Gillibrand, Grey, Hill and Wheatcroft. Others who provided me with necessary factual information include Messrs Draper, Scarlett, Watts and Wilson. All this help saved much tedium and avoided, at least, some errors of fact and emphasis, and I am most grateful to them all. Nevertheless, of course, all opinions expressed remain my own responsibility.

My indebtedness is particularly great to Miss Arkey who typed all the drafts, to Mrs Bigelstone who checked and rechecked the manuscript, and to Dr Barry who tied up all the technical details and advised me throughout. Without their help the idea of writing a book on Airline Marketing would never have got off the ground.

CONTENTS

FIGURES

TABLES

INTRODUCTION

Although all generalisations are questionable since they so frequently over-simplify, there seems to be reasonable ground for the assertion that the older forms of transport had settled down by the turn of the century to providing, on a near-monopolistic basis, a near necessity. Anyone desiring to arrange, for any reason, the carriage of goods or persons sought out the appropriate means of transport. He might have choice between two or three alternative railways or shipping lines; or he might not. Where any competition existed, it was almost universally railway against railway or ship against ship.

True, competition between the alternative carriers was often fierce, and such excitements as the race to the North between the British Railway Companies on the East and West Coast routes were examples of an attempt at product differentiation, with a strong loss leader element, which could fit into any modern marketing pattern.

But all this assumed an over-all demand for the specific kind of service offered. The volume of resources in man-power and money devoted to *creating* demand was minimal. The great transport undertakings of the world, until quite recent times, were staffed and managed by men whose training and inspiration were centred on the operation of a service of high technical and operational efficiency and safety, but who put the function of persuading the public to use these facilities at a relatively low level in the organisation; with appropriately minute financial provision.

The management literature of transport, even today, reflects this technical, operational and analytically economic bias (plus the regulatory aspects), and the newer forms of transport, road and air, do not show up any better in this respect than the older, sea and rail.

There are scores of books on the history, economics and operation of the various forms of transport, very few (and those the most recent) on over-all management problems, and none known to the writer on those aspects of transport management which are today grouped under marketing.

The same bias is reflected in the syllabuses of the examinations of the Institute of Transport, which is the British and Commonwealth professional body for the non-technical (broadly, the non-engineering) transport men. A change in the syllabuses for 1966 introduced 'Management applied to Transport' (which includes marketing) as a compulsory subject for the Associate Membership examination. Let it be made quite clear that this is not because the top transport managers who make up the Council of the Institute have not for some time been conscious of the need, but it is difficult to demand knowledge of a subject in which there is no literature and a paucity of tutors.

The need to hold on to their existing markets, to sell, came home to the railways between the wars with the resurgence of road transport based on the internal combustion engine, and to the shipping companies after the 1939–45 war with the development of the aeroplane capable of trans-ocean flight. Both road and air transport, fighting to win a place for their new facilities against the older established means of transport, have been selling hard, if not always marketing effectively, almost from birth.

The first chapter is taken up with the definition and description of marketing processes in the management complex. But it may be useful to expand here on the other element in the title of this book, namely Air Transport.

In this context Air Transport is defined as a pattern of air services, operating to a published timetable and available for use by members of the public who wish to travel as passengers or to despatch their goods. The services are also open to the carriage of mail. The fares passengers pay and the rates charged for cargo are published.

The other form of commercial air transport is the charter. Here the whole aircraft is hired for the movement of passengers or cargo. The contract may be for one or a series of flights and it will specify times and destinations as required by the charterer. The price will be a matter of negotiation.

Basically this book deals with the first of these, the pattern of time-tabled services, but reference will of necessity be made to charters, particularly in so far as they constitute an important element in the air market for holiday travel.

The object is to relate the principles of good marketing practice to the special circumstances of air transport, and this should have a universal application. There is no difference in the basic marketing *approach* to services between London and Palma, Los Angeles and New York or Addis Ababa and Djibouti.

Markets served, in size and demand characteristics, will vary to an enormous extent, as will the external forces bearing on different operators. The resultant dominant marketing strategies in each case will be quite different. But the principles used to establish the final plan are the same the world over.

CHAPTER I

WHAT IS MARKETING?

To many people marketing is selling and selling is a man with his foot in the door persuading the timid to buy what they neither want nor can afford.

The question of the public image of the salesman and/or the marketing man will be developed at the end of this chapter, but the most useful starting point is to clarify exactly what is meant by marketing.

Any business, whether producing necessities or frivolities, consumer goods, industrial goods or services, has two fundamental functions to perform. It has to produce whatever it is it does produce, and then it has to ensure that those for whom the product is intended get possession of it, normally against payment. In the vast majority of cases in the Western world and, apparently, increasingly in the East, the income from consumers has to meet the production costs, including servicing of the capital employed, otherwise funds cease to be attracted (or directed) to the business and it fails.

In present-day terms, marketing embraces *all* the functions from the end of the production process until the purchase money is taken into the business. And it goes further in that it also includes advice, if no more, on what should be produced, in what numbers and at what price.

There is no standard definition of marketing which is universally accepted. Some definitions are designed to stress particular aspects, others (against the background of the opening paragraph of this chapter) aim at 'selling' the idea of marketing to a suspicious world and a few are carefully thought out to be all-embracing. All need amplification and clarification.

The official definition of the Institute of Marketing of Great Britain looks at marketing as a management control: 'Marketing is the creative management function which promotes trade and employment by assessing consumer needs and initiating research and development to meet them. It co-ordinates the resources of production and distribution of goods and services; determines and directs the

B

nature and scale of the total effort required to sell profitably the maximum production to the ultimate user.' Although the words are different, the same general thought is found in a definition given in an American standard work on marketing:[1] 'The systematic, planned and organised effort needed to find, develop and service the markets for the company's products and to identify and specify the products needed for the company's markets.' Another, by an American marketing consultant (St Thomas) is a useful example of the definition that stresses one aspect, and a very important one at that: 'A way of managing a business so that each critical business decision ... is made with a full fore-knowledge of the impact of that decision on the customer.' Commander Whitehead, the archetype of successful marketers of a British product in the North American market, made the same point in an article in *Marketing*: 'Marketing means matching goods or services to markets ... it means looking at products and problems from the customers' point of view.' Finally, an example of the definition which pleads a case: 'Marketing is the delivery of a standard of living.'

There is no point in subjecting these definitions to a critical appraisal. They are chosen as good examples which, taken together, should at least indicate the broad lines of the subject under discussion. But the important thing about these definitions is that they look at marketing as the driving force in the management of the business. As is commonly said in the consumer goods industries, the only business which can hope to succeed is one that is consumer oriented, producing what it can sell, and the high road to failure is to be production oriented, trying to sell what can be produced.

When one comes to look at the marketing department of a business, it is more detailed in its responsibilities than appears from these definitions and at the same time less authoritative. It, the marketing department, does not directly order the scale and type of production. That is the task of the top management. The point is that the marketing department, as part of its function, will be providing the necessary information on which management can make production decisions and those decisions should be related to, indeed dominated by, the marketing possibilities.

Coming down into detail then, the functions which are grouped together in the marketing complex are:

(*a*) Discovery of what constitutes the market. Who are the potential customers; where are they and how many are there; just what do they want and what will they pay for it; what is the environment (competitive, regulatory, economic) in which the market operates?

---

[1] H. Lazo and A. Corbin, *Management in Marketing*. New York and London: McGraw-Hill, 1961.

All this adds up to market and motivation research and includes advice, from the demand point of view, on price and pricing policies.

(*b*) Feed-back of the results of (*a*) to production. This is the vital function of setting the marketing requirement and so ensuring that what is produced is saleable.

(*c*) Organisation of outlets, the system by which the ultimate customer actually secures possession. This will depend on the practice of the trade and may vary within the trade, but will consist of one or more of the following:—established retail outlets for similar products, agencies, wholesalers, directly owned shops, mail order. This function, exceptionally, may be absent, as in the case of some aspects of industrial marketing such as building railways or nuclear power stations.

(*d*) Distribution. The product or service has to reach the outlet, or the customer, in appropriate quantities and at the required time. Apart from physical movement (or, in the case of a service, ready access) this will involve, for commodities, stockholding and warehousing in order that production flows—probably regular—can be satisfactorily adjusted to meet irregular and/or geographically variable demand patterns.

(*e*) Attraction of the customer *to* the point of sale. This embraces all the range of persuasion covered by advertising, sales promotion, merchandising techniques, outside salesmen, brand image, premium offers, loss leaders (selling one of a range of products below cost to introduce it or the range to the public), and the like.

(*f*) Attraction of the customer *at* the point of sale: point of sale display, packaging, appearance of outlet and staff, etc.

(*g*) Persuasion at the point of sale. This is where selling comes into the marketing picture. It is true that 'selling' as a word is used to describe many other functions. One speaks of an advertisement doing a good selling job for a product. It is useful, however, in looking at the concomitants of marketing, to keep 'selling' as a descriptive term for the actual face to face persuasion which is summed up in the word 'salesmanship'. This process at the point of sale goes just a little further, however, as it includes all aspects necessary to ease the sale, so that credit terms and trade discounts fit into that part of the marketing process.

(*h*) After sales servicing. This does not simply embrace the obvious need, in selling such consumer durables as television sets, to ensure that an adequate servicing and maintenance organisation exists. Even with the simplest of consumer goods the business must be prepared to deal courteously and adequately with complaints. Most businesses live off repeat-selling and also rely to a considerable extent for expansion on word of mouth recommendations by satisfied customers. The sale is, in effect, not the end but the beginning of a relationship with the buyer, and the common sense of this is that the second sale should be easier than the first. The antithesis is the 'foot-in-the-door' salesman, whether literally operating on the door-knocker, through mail-order or in any other way. He is out to make a once-off sale and never appear again. Anybody who still imagines that this typifies salesmanship or selling has only to reflect on the impossibility of well-founded and prosperous businesses which, *in toto*, go to make up the national economies, operating on the basis of such perpetual dissatisfactions. A sale should be like a marriage—neither party should regret it later.

(*i*) The whole process operates in an environment, whatever that may be for the particular business, and not in a vacuum, so the marketing process must include:

(i) Relations with the world at large; in other words public relations;
(ii) Relations with retailers, wholesalers, agents, etc.;
(iii) Relations with appropriate authorities—home Government Departments, foreign Governments, local authorities, trade associations, etc. (even the Mafia or the Tong if their influence operates contiguously);
(iv) Not generally, but occasionally, relations with suppliers;
(v) Relations with competitors.

(*j*) Relations with other functions in the firm. This, of course, is not peculiar to the Marketing Department. All departments have to deal with each other. But it is a matter of special concern to the marketing side, as they will achieve so much more in inclining the firm's corporate thinking towards the requirement they define, if they trouble to use some of the persuasiveness they are paid to direct at potential customers in order to convince their production colleagues. No business can succeed if an unending battle between marketing and production is being constantly arbitrated by the General Manager or Managing Director.

(*k*) In a changing world what is right today as to product, price, market and marketing strategy, may be wrong tomorrow. There must, therefore, be a continuous process of review with the object of developing the existing products, the product line and the market itself.

The *continued* existence of an enterprise is completely dependent on successful adaptation to the changes signalled by the last-mentioned process (*k*). An apt quotation in the context of this book from Theodore Levitt's chapter 'Marketing Myopia', referring to the United States railroads, underlines the lengths to which this process of adaptation may need to go:

'Thus, the railroads did not stop growing because the need for passenger and freight transportation declined. That grew. The railroads are in trouble today not because the need was filled by others (cars, trucks, airplanes, even telephones), but because it was not filled by the railroads themselves. They let others take customers away from them because they assumed themselves to be in the railroad business rather than in the transportation business. The reason they defined this industry wrong was because they were railroad-oriented instead of transportation-oriented; they were product-oriented instead of customer-oriented.'[1]

The relative importance that each of these parts will play in the composite marketing organisation and plan will vary to a considerable degree between products, and even for the same product different firms will have their own ideas as to emphasis. For example, perfume manufacturers may put packaging and point of sale display high on their list; that is, these will predominate in the 'marketing mix', whereas petrol companies may concentrate on national advertising and wholly owned retail outlets. Again, one manufacturer of washing machines may concentrate on retail outlets and another on direct sales by the use of massive coupon advertising. In general, however, it is unusual for any of the basic ingredients (a) to (k) to be altogether absent from a complete marketing operation by a successful business.

The expression 'merchandising' crops up frequently in books on marketing, particularly with reference to consumer goods. Merchandising is, in effect, a particular method of marrying up certain of the elements of marketing. It is best explained by an example. The makers of, say, a chocolate bar sell through a host of retail outlets stocking directly and indirectly competitive lines. They cannot hope for any very positive selling effort by the shop assistant at the point of sale and, anyway, this may be a supermarket where nobody sells anything in the sense that 'selling' is defined in this chapter. Such a manufacturer may well mount a heavy national or local advertising campaign (press, radio or television) using his sales force in good time *before* the campaign appears, to persuade the retailers to stock up because people will be coming in looking for it. To assist in maximising sales the retailer will be persuaded to give the product, or some 'recall' advertising material for it, visual prominence in the shop or supermarket. The whole operation boils down to the manufacturer using the retailer as a stockist, a ready point of access to the eager buyer, rather than a positive seller.

This is the essence of merchandising. The manufacturer or producer is taking all the necessary action to ensure the sale. Because some

---

[1] *Modern Marketing Strategy*, ed. Edward C. Bursk and John F. Chapman, Oxford University Press, 1964.

link in the marketing chain (the retail outlet) is not only not under his control, but is suspect as a positive force, he sells *through* it. A succinct definition is 'obtaining maximum persuasion at the point of sale without personal salesmanship'.[1]

So much for definition and description. But what about the ethos and economics of all this expenditure on persuasion and the machinery for, in many cases, creating demand?

The economic systems of the Western world, even with their variable content of State-owned enterprises, operate on the basis of consumer choice. Moreover, together the consumers in question have massive amounts of expenditure at their disposal for items over and above the fundamentals for keeping alive. The typical consumer is not choosing between fuel to keep warm or food to keep strong, but between two beers or a gin and tonic, a hair-do or the latest nylons, a television set or a continental holiday.

Few of us, relatively, are in the business of providing bare, basic necessities: Even food, clothing and shelter, which are the necessities, are only exceptionally purchased at the lowest of minima. And the fact that the unfortunates who fail in the race can still be supported above these minima (however much argument there may be as to the adequacy of old age pensions or unemployment payments), argues that such societies as ours do 'deliver a standard of living'.

The whole edifice is predicated, therefore, on discretionary expenditure—the choice that is open to Western man and woman as to what he or she does with some part of income. And this choice is not necessarily looking for the cheapest, although like for like (if such comparisons are ever exactly possible), relative cheapness is a powerful factor in choice. High costs may well be accepted for convenience, for example frozen pre-prepared vegetables.

However good or cheap or convenient a product may be, the consumer must be informed and persuaded of the advantages and then he must be put in a position of being able to acquire it easily. This must be achieved, too, in the midst of a clamour of strident voices designed to convince the consumer that his discretionary expenditure should be directed elsewhere; not necessarily to the same type of product which is better, cheaper and more convenient, but to a whole range of quite different products. The growth in wealth of modern societies *affords* more choice, and a primary function of marketing is to reveal this choice.

In passing, because of the range of choice and because persuasion can be coercive or dishonest, consumer protection is a necessary part of the scene. Control of weights and measures, implied warranties of performance, banning of superlative claims in the areas of psychological desperation ('this product will cure cancer') and many others, are

[1] D. W. Smallbone, *Practice of Marketing*, Staples Press, London, 1965.

admitted by any honest marketing man as vitally necessary for his own protection as well as that of the public. Argument only arises over the areas of necessity and practicality.

In essence then, the production side is going to be out of work in the absence of adequate marketing, whilst the marketing side will be in the same sort of trouble if production is not as per agreed specification (quality control, etc.) and as per agreed flow. One cannot over-emphasise the importance of an acceptance within any business of this interdependence.

J. K. Galbraith, particularly in his *Affluent Society*, has written penetratingly on this change from nineteenth-century emphasis on production to twentieth-century emphasis on consumption. In fact he goes so far as to state that output is now so prodigious that the major effort has to be expended on getting rid of it. Even so, this only emphasises the urge to *sell*. Marketing serves the need of the business by doing this, but it sets out to do it most effectively by starting with the consumer requirement and developing new requirements in the process. It reverses the traditional process and works back from the changing pattern of those things which will give consumer satisfaction and then forward again to delivering them.

CHAPTER II

MARKETING A SERVICE

Long before anybody began to think in terms of marketing as an organisational segment of a business, embracing the range of activities already described, some at least of these had of necessity been carried on in most businesses, though rarely integrated. There have always been salesmen, products always had to be distributed, and advertising has a long history. But as a management concept, an approach to the whole way in which the business is run, it owes its development and vitality mainly to the consumer goods industries and, in particular, to the producers of goods which cannot in any sense of the word be described as necessities.

Such firms tend to exhibit the free-for-all environment of the economist's concept of competition, in that no individual business is sufficiently dominant materially to affect the supply on the market by its own expansion or contraction; nor is it able, as a corollary, to control the price level by its own decisions on the amount produced. And this is not only because there are sufficient other producers of the particular product (confectionery, costume jewellery, sandwich fillings) but because even the sole producer of a recondite consumer luxury—say plastic model Eskimo igloos—knows that people don't really need the things and could easily be persuaded to spend their money in other ways; quite apart from the fact that entry into such businesses is often easy, and high profits would soon attract new entrants.

As a result, such businesses have always thrown up managements dominated by marketing considerations, founding all their decisions on the consumer and what he can be persuaded to buy. They have never even had a 'natural' market, such as exists for food, clothing and shelter, which is at least there as a challenge to be entered. The complete market has often to be created. In these circumstances, and spurred on by the economies of size, concentration on marketing both as a management concept and as a combination of techniques has been, and is, vital to such industries.

All this, of course, has spilled over into firms which are not producers of consumer luxuries and whose products range from industrial goods such as machinery to consumer necessities such as bread. The service industries, in turn, have begun to move in the same direction. As was indicated in the previous chapter, the importance of the different ingredients in the marketing plan—the mix—will show great variations.

As soon as one looks at the problems of marketing a service, however, the mix—and in particular the relationship between production and marketing—has to take into account a fundamental characteristic that differentiates tangible products from services.

Ignoring bespoke production, and accepting that batch production is also somewhat special, the typical business decision to market a tangible product consists in its simplest terms of: scanning the market, deciding on style and quality, and setting up production at an annual rate which (at the price determined by forecast demand on the one hand and forecast costs on the other) is expected to be absorbed by the market and adequately remunerate capital employed, that is, show a profit. The technical marketing process, if the decision-making has been sound, then converts this expectation into reality.

Inherent in this process are several consistent features:

(a) Production will probably be organised on a regular flow basis—so many units a day every day—because this is almost certain to be the way to secure the lowest costs. Seasonal demand irregularities will be ironed out by storage.

(b) Given sound decision-making in this respect, fluctuations in the pattern of demand will be met at no greater cost penalty than that of storing excess production when demand is low.

(c) Price, in these conditions, over time will reflect average cost; that is, in the same market no unit will be, or can be, on sale *habitually* at more or less than another unit. Surpluses may be cleared off by lowering the cost of *all* units at the same time (the 'sale' technique). Admittedly market imperfections may at times permit different prices *for exactly the same product* to exist even in the same High Street, but the tendency will always be for such situations to rectify themselves.

(d) If decision-making has not been sound, or if conditions change so that supply and demand diverge and price moves above or below average cost, decisions (including movement of new firms into, and existing firms out of, the market) will be taken to achieve the equilibrium described, by means of a new level of even flow prices which, over time, will equate demand at acceptable prices.

(e) If the factory is efficiently organised, with adequate quality control and inspection, each unit will be exactly the same and agree precisely with the specification, which will correspond in detail with what the marketing side is offering. On the rare occasion when this is not so—a faulty article slipping through inspection—on complaint the customer can usually be satisfied by changing the defective product for one that is not faulty.

A service of any kind, since it does not consist of delivering a tangible product to the customer, cannot be organised in this way, with consequent effects on costs, prices, and the extent to which production can be bent towards the market requirement.

Although this is true of all services, from surgery to window-cleaning, the effects are most clearly seen in the highly organised and complex structure of a transport undertaking.

If demand for passenger travel is twice as heavy in summer as it is in winter, even flow production through the year, taking the excess winter production off the shelves in summer, is impossible. Production can be varied to an extent, without substantial cost increases, to meet demand fluctuations. For example, in the case of air transport such items as crew training and aircraft modifications can be concentrated in the demand trough period. But the scope for this is actually very limited and, in any case, demand is not on a low plateau all winter and a high plateau all summer. The real problem is the trough in the trough (perhaps November or February in British conditions) and the peak of the peak, which in Britain is probably August. If these extreme demand fluctuations are considerable unit cost will rise fiercely if production is tailored to meet them all.

To illustrate this point the following figures are taken from an actual exercise (that is, not a theoretical one), in which comparison was made between the economics of a short-haul operation mounting five services daily throughout the year, and the same operation having five daily in the seven summer months, but only two daily in the five winter months. In the former case the average cost per round trip, including overheads and everything, was £1,021. In the second case, using the same methods of cost allocation, it was £1,250. The number of passengers at current fares required to break even on costs was sixty-six compared with eighty-one, or in load factor terms (the percentage of paying load compared with total saleable load), the break-even factor in the 'even flow' case was 52 per cent, whereas it was 64 per cent where winter frequencies were reduced, the aircraft containing 126 seats.

This does not mean, of course, that the schedule actually operated was five a day all the year round, because although this reduces unit cost, the *total* annual costs of the whole operation are greater (in this case by some £150,000) and if the traffic is not forthcoming in the winter to provide *at least* that much extra revenue, then it is better to operate the reduced winter programme.

In circumstances such as these price variations appear. The detailed aspects of pricing are developed in Chapter VI. The general point made here is that the special characteristics of a service, and of a transport service in particular, make pricing (fares or rates policy) a much more complex and flexible marketing tool than is the case with commodities. Services between the same places at different times of the year, on different days of the week and even at different times of the day, are usually quite different products from the point of view of demand. Viewed in this light, it is not surprising that different fares are charged for what may appear on the surface to be the same product, an airline seat between A and B.

From the marketing point of view, however, particularly when dealing with passenger fares, the variations in the published fares for the same journey at different periods are not merely reflections of the inability to store. Intelligently devised, such fare variations can be a potent weapon to persuade traffic away from the peaks at least into the shoulder periods (those on either side of the peak) if not actually into the troughs. Success in this respect not only gets more traffic into the shoulders, albeit at a lower price for all the traffic carried during these periods, and removes the worst pressure at the peak, but also by smoothing out demand enables production to be smoothed out to the same extent, thus reducing costs.

Finally there is one more fundamental difference between a commodity and a service. The supply of the service is highly personalised. Provided a suite of furniture is exactly what the purchaser expected for his money he does not care—indeed does not know— what sort of people made it. The use he gets out of the furniture is the sole satisfaction he is seeking for his money. But in the case of a service, the attitude and even the appearance of the person or persons performing that service affect the satisfaction the customer gets for his money.

It goes further than that. Bad workmanship in a factory can be corrected on inspection or, if it slips through, in most cases put right by replacement. Turning to transport as an example of a service for the contrast, an inefficient link in the chain of people involved in the complete journey or cargo movement can irretrievably ruin the whole product. Moreover, replacement is not possible. If a holiday is spoiled, a business appointment missed, or an urgent order fails to arrive on time, the offer of a free ride or free carriage at a later date is no recompense. Apart from the inadequacy of such an offer, there is the added difficulty that, whereas it is reasonably easy in most cases to decide whether an object is faulty, it is seldom possible to judge with any accuracy how far a particular spoilt journey's departure from specification merits 'replacement'.

This whole question of the attitude and competence of staff in touch with the public is of paramount concern when considering transport marketing, and will be described further in a later chapter.

CHAPTER III

SPECIAL FEATURES OF AIR TRANSPORT

The previous chapter brought out the salient differences between commodities, that is tangible objects of all kinds, and services. Although air transport situations were used in illustrating the argument, examples could as well have been drawn from other service industries.

The purpose of this analysis is to build up the necessary limiting or conditioning factors which affect marketing, and this chapter is designed to complete the picture by describing the additional features which distinguish air transport from other service industries.

Firstly, a peculiarity shared with all forms of transport, the service which air transport provides is not desired for itself. The passengers, the cargo and the mail do not want a ride in an aeroplane; what they want is to be at their destination. The journey is no more than a time-consuming, costly but essential purchase to overcome the disability of separation which inhibits the attainment of the real objective. Moreover, in the case of cargo, air transport (and again all transport) not only is not wanted for itself, but is often part of the marketing costs of its customers, under the heading of 'Distribution'.

Secondly, and this is particularly true of air transport, the product is frequently undifferentiated. That is to say, in a great many cases the offer by ABC Airlines is in every essential respect—including price—the same as that offered by XYZ Airlines. If several carriers are operating a transatlantic flight between the same points, at the same fare, using the same aircraft type, at times of day of equal convenience, it takes the loving eye of an advertising man to bring out the advantages one has over the other. Even where conditions are not so exactly paralleled as in this example, true differences do tend to be small.

Thirdly, one must mention weather, which affects all transport but bears particularly hard on air transport. Technical improvements in flying and navigation aids tend to improve the situation all the time, but, particularly in certain areas—of which Europe is one—bad weather can thoroughly disorganise the product. This is more of a genuine sales deterrent than a factor determining marketing methods, but anybody who has ever had to build up traffic for an airline during bad weather seasons knows that this factor does affect sales emphasis, if no more.

But the outstanding peculiarity of air transport lies in the area of external controls. Practically all transport, being part of the economic infra-structure of trade and industry, operates under some sort of Government control, and it is the form, extent and strength of these controls, from case to case, that affect individual marketing practice.

For the purpose in hand, one can ignore the stringent regulations designed to ensure safety, and even such controls as limitation or banning of night flights to minimise noise disturbance to residents near airports. All these controls raise costs, which means higher prices, which limits market expansion. But they do not have an influence on method.

In what follows, only sufficient detail is given to bring into the picture those features which affect marketing. The full aspects and implications of Government control of airline operation can be found elsewhere. Anybody concerned with the commercial aspects of civil aviation is well advised to read the full texts of the Air Services Agreements concluded by his country, as well as of any laws or regulations affecting freedom to operate, such as licensing regulations; and, it goes without saying, to keep himself up-to-date in this respect, not only by staying abreast of change, but by reading the literature which constantly appears as a commentary on this aspect of the aviation scene.[1]

The controls which curtail the freedom of action of airlines operating international services, however much they differ in important detail, have one thing in common. All these operations are governed by bilateral Air Services Agreements made between sovereign Governments. In the absence of such an agreement, whether enshrined in a comprehensive formal document, published as a White Paper (or the equivalent), or in a temporary exchange of Notes pending a formal agreement, no international air transport is possible.

Basically from the marketing point of view, these agreements normally permit the air operators of Country A and Country B to fly and carry paying load between Country A and Country B (these being the contracting parties), over a route network specifically defined in an Annexe to the agreement. In the language of the Chicago Convention on Civil Aviation of 1944, which also set up the International Civil Aviation Organisation (ICAO) to which all air-faring nations adhere, we are now in the realm of the 'Freedoms'.

[1] For example, Stephen Wheatcroft's *Air Transport Policy*. London: Michael Joseph, 1964.

As defined by the Chicago Convention, these are:

First: The privilege of flying across a country without landing.

Second: The privilege of landing for non-traffic purposes.

Third: The privilege of putting down passengers, mail and freight taken on board in the territory of the State whose nationality the aircraft bears.

Fourth: The privilege of taking up passengers, mail and freight destined for the territory of the State whose nationality the aircraft bears.

Fifth: The privilege of taking on passengers, mail and freight destined for the territory of a State other than that whose nationality the aircraft bears, and the privilege of putting down passengers, mail and freight taken on board in such territory.

One more Freedom, which does not appear in the Chicago Convention, but which is of considerable importance to certain airlines because of their geographical position, is the so-called Sixth Freedom. This is the right of the airline of Country B to carry traffic from Country A, *through* Country B to Country C.

Cabotage traffic is that which begins and ends its journey within the territory of a single State. Rights to carry this traffic are almost never given to an airline other than one registered in the State concerned, although exceptionally the general rule is broken by an undeveloped State which has not yet got its own airline (usually in return for some other benefit, such as money).

These Freedoms can perhaps best be understood by re-defining them in terms of the national airline of a sovereign power—Midstate Airlines—which operates services to the neighbouring self-governing countries of Northstate and Southstate, and also through Southstate to Farsouthstate.

The traffic that Midstate Airlines picks up in Midstate and carries to Northstate, Southstate or Farsouthstate as its respective destinations, is Third Freedom traffic. Traffic it carries from any of these three countries which terminates its journey in Midstate, is Fourth Freedom traffic. In the language of the 'White House Statement on International Air Transport Policy—April 1963', which outlined the United States Government's thinking on international air transport regulation, these two kinds of traffic constitute primary justification traffic.

Reverting to Midstate Airlines, any traffic it picks up in Southstate and carries to Farsouthstate, and vice versa, is Fifth Freedom traffic. Traffic picked up in Northstate and taken *through* Midstate to either Southstate or Farsouthstate or vice versa, would be so-called Sixth Freedom traffic. These, the White House statement already mentioned calls secondary justification traffic.

Traffic beginning and terminating its journey completely within Midstate would be cabotage traffic for Midstate Airlines.

Although the authorisation of Third and Fourth Freedom operation to the airlines of both States is the common nub of Air Services Agreements, the freedom to operate in an unrestricted manner, using such Freedoms, is more often curtailed than not, even for this primary justification traffic.

Where the two national airlines are mature and strong, the agreement will usually be written in such a way as to ensure fair and equal opportunity for the airlines of both States.[1] This does not mean that each party must provide exactly 50 per cent of the 'required' capacity, whatever that may mean. It does imply, however, that the operator who puts on sufficient capacity to carry *all* the traffic offering both ways at a low load factor would almost certainly, in European conditions as well as many others, find itself cut back, on an *ex post facto* review, by the *other* Government concerned.

However, even so far as primary justification traffic is concerned, particular agreements, or the permissions which derive from them, can be very restrictive. This particularly arises where the airline of one of the States is weak, or still developing. Whether the agreement is written in such a way that the capacity offered has to be predetermined from time to time by the Governments, or that the two national airlines have to agree in advance of each scheduling period, or any variation on the same theme, the effect is the same—to restrict the freedom to operate of one of the carriers more than it would be in the case of a Bermuda type agreement. Even a Bermuda type agreement can, from time to time, be interpreted restrictively by one of the parties to it.

When we look at the Fifth and Sixth Freedoms (secondary justification traffic), the situation is highly restrictive. The Fifth is increasingly allowed purely on a bargaining basis, and the period since the late 1950's has been characterised by more and more examples of airlines, with existing Fifth Freedom rights, having them curtailed because their own Governments were unable to offer to

---

[1] In 1946 Great Britain and the USA signed an agreement in Bermuda 'relating to Air Services between their respective territories' (Cmd. 6747, 1946). This agreement has been used as a model for many others, and so the phrase has grown up 'a Bermuda type agreement'. This states, *inter alia*, 'there shall be a fair and equal opportunity for the carriers of the two nations to operate on any route . . . covered by the agreement. . . . That, in the operation by the air carriers of either Government of the trunk services . . . the interest of the air carriers of the other Government shall be taken into consideration so as not to affect unduly the services which the latter provides on all or part of the same routes.'

the airline of the curtailing State, similar rights in their own gift which could be considered of compensating commercial value.[1]

Agreements tend to be silent on the Sixth Freedom, but an airline which concentrates on developing this kind of traffic can expect eventually to meet obstacles of some kind. In a controlled situation, such as universally exists, Sixth Freedom traffic can prove a serious leak. Theoretically, as the Air Services Agreements control Third and Fourth Freedom capacity, substantial Sixth Freedom traffic would swell the total traffic of the airline carrying it, and the resultant capacity, being judged solely on the terms of the agreement relating to the Third and Fourth, could be regarded as excessive and prejudicing the principle of 'fair and equal opportunity'. If any airline wanted its Government to intervene against a heavy Sixth Freedom carrier, this is the weapon it would use.

Whatever the details of particular agreements, the over-all picture is clear. In general, the markets to be served and the amount of production put on to satisfy them are controlled by Governments. In almost no case of real traffic importance is any international carrier free to go after such markets as interest it with as much productive capacity as it feels disposed to operate.

The agreements normally leave it to the contracting parties to nominate their carriers. In many countries of the world, so far as scheduled services are concerned, the practice is to nominate *one* national carrier. There are important exceptions, the United States, Great Britain and France being outstanding in this respect. The USA, apart from having several different international carriers, also tends towards nomination of two carriers on the same routes, though only if traffic is heavy on such routes. Great Britain and France are also inclined to give different routes to different carriers, although after the Civil Aviation (Licensing) Act of 1960, Great Britain moved slightly towards the United States system of dual designation for the same heavy traffic route.

[1] A Bermuda type agreement has a general, but not very specific, form of control. '. . . services provided by a designated air carrier . . . shall retain as their primary objective the provision of capacity adequate to the traffic demands between the country of which such carrier is a national and the country of ultimate destination of the traffic. The right to embark or disembark on such services international traffic destined for and coming from third countries at a point or points on the routes specified . . . shall be applied in accordance with the general principles of orderly development to which both Governments subscribe and shall be subject to the general principle that capacity should be related:

(*a*) to traffic requirements between the country of origin and the countries of destination.

(*b*) to the requirement of through airline operation; and

(*c*) to the traffic requirement of the area through which the airline passes after taking account of local and regional services.'

C

The effect of all this is that an international scheduled air carrier will find itself very exceptionally a monopolist on a route, usually operating in parallel with at least one other carrier and, because of dual designation and Fifth Freedom operations, sometimes in competition with several direct carriers. In practically all cases, indirect operators operating on a Sixth Freedom basis offer additional competition to the direct carriers.

Turning from control of markets and production to control of prices, the normal bilateral Air Services Agreement between States reserves to the contracting powers final control over the fares and rates to be charged. Either specifically in the agreement, or as a matter of practice, the powers invariably accept the rate-fixing machinery of the International Air Transport Association, subject to an overriding authority to accept or reject agreements that emerge from this machinery.

This leads to the role of the International Air Transport Association (IATA). This body, formed in 1945, is the trade association of the international scheduled air carriers, with almost complete membership except (at the time of writing) for the Russian, Communist Chinese, and most—but not all—other airlines of the Communist States. The possibility of Aeroflot, the USSR airline, joining is by no means remote, which could bring in those other countries in communion with Moscow.

IATA performs many functions, but for the purpose of this book the one that matters is its activity, through what are called the Traffic Conferences, in setting tariffs. These embrace the levels of rates and fares (but not air mail rates) and all related provisions, in particular relating to the standards that may be offered for the agreed fares. Agreements reached in these Conferences cover every international fare and rate used by Members and the conditions attached thereto (thus effectively covering the world). They have to be reached unanimously and they are binding. Because of the highly advantageous position gained by any Members quietly ignoring these agreements after they have been made, a system of inspection has been set up with enforcement by heavy financial penalties for infringements.

As stated earlier, usually through wording in the Air Services Agreements, Governments whose airlines are members of IATA accept this machinery with a right of veto on any, all or parts of these agreements. With occasional notable exceptions, most States most of the time do not, in fact, exercise this right.

So we really have a situation where the States themselves start with the *right* to agree the tariffs between themselves, often expressly so stated in the Air Services Agreements, but leave the negotiating and bargaining to their airlines, using the IATA Traffic Conference machinery, always subject to final acceptance by the sovereign authority. It is worth stressing this. IATA is not a cosy price-fixing body. It is a composite instrument whereby the interests of all its Members *and* the final authority of the appropriate Governments have to come together to set the price levels of international scheduled air transport.

It is much less easy to outline any kind of general picture of the regulatory aspects of air transport operations entirely confined to the territory of one sovereign State, that is, cabotage operations, because these vary so much from country to country. It is, however, reasonably correct to say that where such domestic operations are commercially feasible in the light of distance, terrain, existing communications and potential traffic, so that enterprises begin to cater for the domestic air transport market, some kind of Government control inevitably follows.

In some cases a national carrier may be given a monopoly; in others some machinery exists to choose the carriers, assign routes to them, control any resulting competition that may arise and rule on fares and rates. This latter category embraces most of the really important domestic networks in the non-Communist world, for example the United States, Australia, Great Britain and Japan.

These systems vary widely because of accidents of history or, perhaps more important, differences in national philosophies. As this is not a book on regulatory systems as such, however, no attempt will be made to describe and compare them. Fundamentally the situation that emerges in every case is the same as for international carriage. Air transport undertakings are rarely free to go after markets in their own country at will, or to charge what fares and rates they like once they are in business. The degree of control or freedom in each particular case will condition the approach to market development and tariff-setting at least, and sometimes to product development (for example in Australia where the 'two airline policy' prevents one equipping with more advanced aircraft before the other). The whole field of public relations activity designed to condition public opinion at large (and so, in the end, the decisions of the public's elected representatives forming the Government) will be very much coloured by the position of a particular domestic carrier *vis-à-vis* others.

This aspect of public relations and a Government's attitudes towards its own airlines raises the whole issue of nationalisation, again, from the point of view of this book, solely as it affects the marketing situation.

The ownership of airlines varies very much throughout the world; airlines range from completely private enterprises to those which are wholly State-owned, with many variations in between embodying a mixture of State and private capital (sometimes with a third element, Regional Government capital, also engaged).

Some wholly State-owned airlines are very much instruments of Government policy, 'carrying the flag' without too much regard for the cost, and allowed to suffer no competition from other airlines registered in the State. On the face of it, marketing as such has little place in management thinking where this situation exists. However, there is no such thing as a monopoly in international carriage, so that such an airline, if it wants to carry any traffic at all, must enter foreign markets with the same marketing instruments used by its competitors.

More typical of the wholly or partially State-owned international operators is one that, though it may have a monopoly or near-monopoly of the scheduled operations flown under its national flag, is at the same time expected to pay its way. Typical examples of major airlines in this situation are SAS (the joint airline of Norway, Denmark and Sweden), KLM (Holland) and Swissair. The same is also true of the British State Corporations, BEA and BOAC. In their case their former monopoly of British flag international scheduled services has disappeared since the 1960 Civil Aviation (Licensing) Act. Nor is this situation confined to the international scene. BEA in its British domestic operations, Trans Australian Airways within Australia, and others, meet the competition of private enterprises and are expected to be profitable.

In general terms, whatever the ownership of an airline, provided it is expected to cover its costs and remunerate capital, its marketing management emphasis and general marketing approach will be the same.

Since this is often doubted by those who earn their living, whether in aviation or out of it, in the milieu of competitive private enterprise, it is perhaps worth while to expand a little on the previous paragraph.

An airline, whether State-owned or not, will legally be an entity of some kind—a State Corporation, a company with limited liability—and as such will be regarded, in law, as performing certain acts. But the fact still remains that an airline, as a decision-making business, is composed of people. Starting from the top, the most senior full-time professional, whether he be called Chairman, President, Chief Executive or anything else, holds his appointment from the appropriate Minister of the Government of the day.

As was said earlier, the typical important airline wholly or partially State-owned is expected to pay its way. For example, BEA and BOAC in this respect are covered by the policy expressed in Cmd 1337, 1961, 'The Financial and Economic Obligations of the Nationalised Industries'. Relevant extracts are '. . . although the industries have obligations of a national and non-commercial kind, they are not, and ought not, to be regarded as social services absolved from economic and commercial justification' and 'The undertakings have, in common parlance, been expected to pay their way. . . .' The White Paper indicated that each industry would be set a target of profitability, after providing for depreciation and reserves, on a five-year basis. Each case would be considered in relation to the particular 'wider obligations' borne by it compared with commercial concerns in the private sector.

The target eventually set for BEA was an average of 6 per cent on the capital employed over the five years beginning 1963–64. BOAC, in deep financial trouble at the time, was not given such a target, but later had a capital reorganisation which included an equity element as part of its totally Government-provided stock.

BOAC's troubles cost its Chairman, Chief Executive and several Board Members their appointments. The new Chairman announced a redundancy programme. This unhappy incident demonstrates as clearly as anything could that the man or men at the top have to run a commercially successful concern, and the professionals below them at all levels will also only hold their jobs and advance in their careers if they operate commercially. Which, in a tough world of alternative outlets for discretionary expenditure, means that the whole enterprise has to be consumer oriented—marketing conscious.

Moreover, the path of the commercial airline is made no easier by the existence of the others with less compulsion in this direction. Almost no country is ready to face a situation where losses force its own air transport undertakings out of business. The adjustment of supply, in a situation of over-supply, by bankruptcy is almost unknown in international air transport. This feature makes the task of satisfying share-holders and/or Ministers even more difficult, since the normally efficient concern cannot rely on the market adjusting itself by the disappearance of the inefficient in bad times.

To summarise, air transport, both international and domestic, operates throughout the world under a variety of external controls which limit freedom of action. Although these controls may differ widely from case to case, the *typical* situation is one of control. These controls are of the same generic kind as have been developed for other forms of transport (particularly railways but very much less so for shipping), but are quite special to air transport. Again, in very varying degrees, individual airlines receive some protection from competition from other airlines. A measure of protection is typical.

Whatever the form or extent of control, all this limits the scope of the marketing process; it can never inhibit its necessity. Protection, rarely giving monopoly, normally producing semi-monopoly (or, more precisely, oligopoly, to use one of the economist's uglier descriptive terms) can still only limit the number of players in the air transport game. It cannot regulate the over-all demand for air transport,[1] and this demand is elastic, liable to grow with reducing prices and good marketing and stagnate with rising prices and inefficient marketing.

[1] Except theoretically so far as domestic air transport is concerned; a State could enforce artificially high or low fares and rates domestically, and this would have an effect on demand. In the Western world, such artificial price structures are, to say the least, uncommon.

CHAPTER IV

THE MARKET FOR AIR TRANSPORT

Air transport, in common with other forms of transport, enables people and things to change location. So far as people are concerned, the desire to use the service provided will spring from one of three quite different reasons (even though at times, but fairly exceptionally, the same journey may be motivated by more than one of these reasons). They are:

(a) Pleasure, that is to say, essentially holiday-making.

(b) Business.

(c) Personal—this is quite separate from (a) since, for example, it includes such objectives as attending funerals! It is important to differentiate this personal travel from pleasure travel, since it frequently has a compulsion as to date or place which is absent in the holiday market.

Inanimate objects for which senders will pay air carriage divide between cargo and mail. The former, while it can be subdivided logically into several categories for marketing purposes, is overwhelmingly connected with trade. That is to say cargo moves because of commercial transactions tied to dates and places. As noted in an earlier chapter, these movements are in effect the distribution aspect of the marketing processes of manufacturers and trading concerns.

Mail consists, of course, of both letters and parcels (and the latter may be cargo). But the important point is that the post is a service universally offered under monopoly conditions by State organs, and will only move by air if Post Office authorities so decide.

By any mass transport standards, the contribution that air transport makes to the total movement of passengers, cargo and mail is trivial, but this is because total movement is swollen by the massive volume of local and short distance movements for which air transport does not cater. Where long and very long distances are involved, air transport has become important relative to surface transport as far as total movement of passengers and mail is concerned, but this is not yet true of cargo in general.

From the marketing point of view, the important questions are—
how big is the existing market? What are the possibilities of growth
(development)?

In general, world-wide terms, the total international and domestic
traffic carried by the 107 ICAO contracting States (major exclusions
are USSR and People's Republic of China) is a fair measure of total
volume. The figures are given in Table 1.

TABLE 1. *Volume of traffic carried by ICAO Contracting States in 1965*

	Millions
Passengers carried	180
Passenger-kilometres	199,000
Cargo tonne-kilometres	5,010
Mail tonne-kilometres	1,050

Table 2 illustrates the growth rates over the preceding seven years:

TABLE 2. *Growth in volume of traffic carried by ICAO Contracting States 1958–65*

	1958–59	1959–60	1960–61	1961–62	1962–63	1963–64	1964–65
Passengers	+13%	+ 8%	+ 5%	+ 9%	+12%	+15%	+16%
Passenger-kms.	+14%	+12%	+ 7%	+11%	+13%	+16%	+16%
Cargo tonne-kms.	+16%	+12%	+14%	+18%	+12%	+20%	+28%
Mail tonne-kms.	+11%	+17%	+18%	+11%	+ 8%	+ 6%	+15%

In *total* tonne-kilometre terms, traffic more than doubled between 1958 and 1964.

But, of course, the only meaningful approach to the actual
possibilities and problems of marketing air transport is to examine
particular markets, with their variations in population density,
average income per head, industrial and commercial development,
etc.

Where industrial and commercial development has progressed to
a considerable degree, with its concomitants of high average wealth,
air travel already commands a substantial proportion of the existing
passenger market. For example, between the United Kingdom and
the Continent of Europe, by 1963–64 just over half the passengers
were moving by air, whilst on the North Atlantic routes between
Europe and North America the percentage was even higher (some
85 per cent). In 1963, three passengers went abroad by air from the
USA for every one that travelled by sea. In 1964 over 55 per cent
of all domestic inter-city common carrier passenger miles in the USA
were performed by air.

Another way of assessing the importance of the existing air
transport market is to look at the revenues earned by representative

airlines. In the year 1964–65 British Overseas Airways earned £114 million (US $320 million) in operating revenue, the figure for British European Airways being £66 million (US $185 million).

In the United States, the eleven major domestic carriers had annual traffic revenue in 1964 totalling $2,800 (American) billion, and the over-all traffic revenue of the whole United States scheduled airline industry, domestic and international, was half as large again ($4,250 billion). In Australia, the two major domestic carriers, Trans Australian Airlines and Ansett ANA, earned £A54 million (US $121 million) in 1964–65, and Japan Airlines, principally an international carrier, had an annual revenue of 47,103 million yen (US $130 million) in the same year.

These somewhat random figures are merely designed to show that, by the mid-sixties, the airline industry had grown to major proportions. Moreover, since the volume of air movement in the years immediately preceding the 1939–45 war was minimal, and civil flying in many parts of the world was virtually non-existent during the war, growth to this position has actually been concentrated into no more than twenty years.

This is demonstrated in Table 3 by the ICAO figures for 1945, in comparison to the 1965 figures in Table 1.

TABLE 3. *Comparison of volume of traffic carried by ICAO Contracting States in 1945 and 1965*

	1945 millions	1965 millions
Passengers carried	9	180
Passenger-kilometres	8,000	199,000
Cargo tonne-kilometres	110	5,010
Mail tonne-kilometres	130	1,050

Throughout, the dominant contributor to airline revenues is passenger traffic. For example, of British European Airways' total traffic revenue in 1964–65, 87 per cent came from passengers and their baggage. The equivalent BOAC figure was 76 per cent. In 1964 82 per cent of all United States airlines' revenue came from passenger traffic. The world-wide ICAO figure for 1963 (latest available) was 78 per cent.

Growth in passenger air travel up to this point has been achieved in the following ways:

(*a*) Straight diversion from existing surface traffic.

(*b*) New business and personal journeys made possible or attractive by speed.

(*c*) New holiday journeys made possible (because of distance and time available) by speed, or attractive through a combination of speed and comfort.

(*d*) New journeys of all kinds made possible as the 'affordability' of an air journey increases with rising wealth and reduction in the real cost of air travel.

(*e*) General growth due to rising population and increased trade.

It is probable that future growth in developed countries will come less and less from diversion. Apart from the fact that in many depth markets (e.g. across the English Channel, transatlantic, between major cities in North America, the United Kingdom, Australia and Japan) penetration by air is already very deep, two main forces are likely to slow down any further diversion.

Firstly, all airlines in the twenty years of post-war development have been able to reap the cost-reducing advantages of:

(*a*) Expansion, giving the economies of size, not available to the small units typical (even in the United States) of the early years.

(*b*) Technical development, which has been enormous.

(*c*) Developing airline and management expertise or know-how.

So far as (*a*) is concerned, this has slowed down already. In fact there are those who speculate on the possibility that some airlines are beyond the optimum size and are now in the phase of dis-economies.

The twenty years since 1945 have seen the transition from the small piston-engine aeroplane to the large jet. Most speculation as to the next stage (supersonic) seems to imply that this will give speed advantages but not unit cost savings—in fact possibly the reverse. And in any case this is many years away. Again, vertical take-off machines still produce capacity ton miles at costs above fixed wing aircraft, and improvements come very slowly in this direction. Improvements in component life and other aspects of engineering costs appear to offer less scope than previously for dramatic savings. Traffic growth enabling larger aircraft to be sensibly used still offers opportunities for load-ton-mile cost savings, but again perhaps less universally than previously.

On the other hand, as traffic grows, the complexity and sophistication of air traffic control and navigation aids are causing costs to rise. The necessity, as saturation of existing busy airports is reached, of splitting operations between more than one airport in order to serve major cities, will cause general airline costs to rise independently. Operating techniques to minimise the noise nuisance, coupled with such controls as limitations on night flying, are also likely to increase costs in the future.

All in all, although it would be madness to base predictions on a view that the technical honeymoon is over, it does seem that unit costs arising from these aspects of aviation are, at the very least, unlikely to continue to fall steeply. Indeed, one could argue the probability that advances in technology may be off-set by the kind of trend mentioned in the preceding paragraph, so that, at best, airline technical and operating costs in total will move in line with general costs (wages, materials, etc.).

As for airline and management ability, the industry is now bedded down into a pattern of skill and experience built up over a single generation, each member of whom had to learn as he went along. The second and later generations will undoubtedly improve on what has gone before, but as in the other fields of earlier cost reduction, the scope for anything dramatic is undoubtedly lessening—the curve will flatten out.

The object of this far from profound—and perhaps controversial— analysis is to indicate that the rate of diversion from surface transport, due to falling real cost of air transport relative to the real cost of surface transport, is likely to slow down considerably in developed countries. However, in densely populated poor countries the potential is still great as *per capita* wealth increases.

The second force likely to reduce the rate of diversion is the increasing tendency of surface carriers to fight back. The long delayed improvement in the Melbourne–Sydney rail link, overcoming a break of gauge problem that had existed ever since the different Australian States had built their railways without a common gauge, is one example. The speeding up and improvement of the rail service Tokyo–Osaka is another. Other, less noteworthy improvements of various kinds in railway service throughout the world, are typical of the sixties. Similarly, ocean shipping, unable to do anything useful to close the speed gap, has concentrated on selling its 'rest, relax, and recuperate' advantages, and experimented with class and berth categorisations to meet changing market requirements. The air cushion (hovercraft) vehicle is in its infancy, and developments such as the channel tunnel will alter the terms of air/surface competition in particular markets.

Although the air carriers can, therefore, perhaps look less and less in future to existing surface traffic as a source from which to maintain their own growth, the prospects of expansion from the development of entirely new traffic are, to say the least, encouraging.

So far as passenger travel is concerned, the cash for that part of it which is pleasure or personal comes out of the population's discretionary expenditure—that part of income which is not committed to the standard of essentials which each individual works out for himself (plus taxation!). In the developed countries with their already high standard of living, and its substantial 'non-essential' content, every addition to *per capita* wealth, as economic expansion goes forward, is available for further expenditure on goods and services which make life pleasanter rather than merely more tolerable. All the evidence of the post-war years, which have seen such a tremendous increase in the *number* of people in developed countries with incomes well above subsistence standard, indicates that travel is a highly favoured outlet for some part of discretionary expenditure. For example, between 1950 and 1960, when total consumer expenditure in the United Kingdom rose by 75 per cent, the foreign travel element increased by 140 per cent. Similar figures for the United States were 70 and 170 per cent.

The graphs in figure 1, shown opposite, bring out quite clearly the way in which expenditure on foreign travel has grown faster than total consumer expenditure in the United Kingdom and the United States.

The trend for expenditure on non-essentials to grow faster than total expenditure will undoubtedly continue in the developed societies, and should emerge in the under-developed as they progress. As an example, it has been calculated that in the United Kingdom between 1964 and 1974, total consumer expenditure will increase by some 35 per cent, whereas the luxury (non-essential) content of this growth will go up by over 55 per cent. There is every reason to believe that travel expenditure, and particularly air travel expenditure, will (as in the past) increase even faster.

The potential can be gauged from some figures given in a booklet called *A Profile of the Air Traveller* published by American Airlines in December 1963, and which resulted from a survey which is claimed to be 'the equivalent of the yield from a national probability sample of 25,000 people'.

For this purpose, the important findings are:

(*a*) That 50 per cent of American air travellers are on business, 35 per cent on pleasure journeys, and the remaining 15 per cent move for non-leisure personal reasons.

(*b*) Of the American population over 18 years of age, 10 per cent travelled by air in the year of the survey, and nearly 30 per cent had done so at some time or other.

The United States is the leading 'consumer society' and yet these figures show that, as yet, really quite a small proportion buy air travel out of personal income.

The implications of these figures, plus the future possibilities inherent in the progress of the heavily populated under-developed nations, points to pleasure and personal travel, and air travel in particular, being a strong growth market for as far ahead as one can reasonably foresee. This, of course, still leaves unresolved the percentage the scheduled airlines can gain against the growth of holidays by charter aircraft.

EXPENDITURE ON FOREIGN TRAVEL v TOTAL CONSUMER EXPENDITURE 1950-1963.

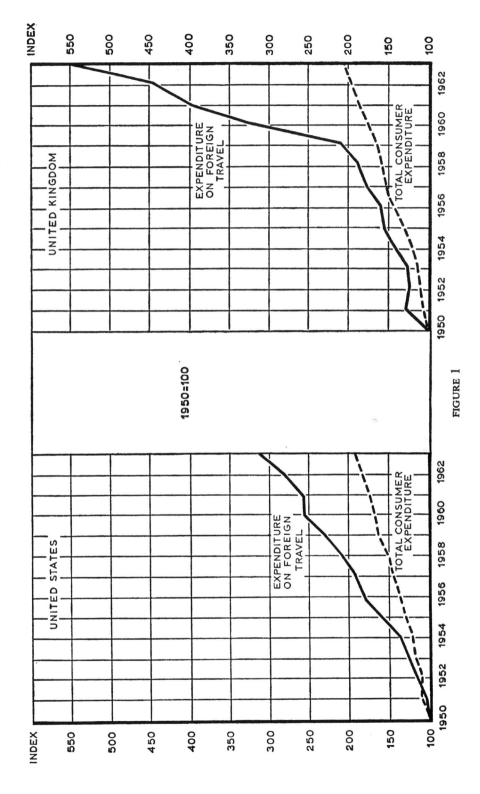

FIGURE 1

The business air travel market, in turn, has its own built-in growth factors. The mutual reaction of increasing trade and personal incomes leads to more journeys *in support of* the greater volume of business, whilst the improvement in communications and growth in size and number of firms leads to more journeys *in search of* business.

A growth point in business travel that has considerable potential is in the lower income range of business men, often a salesman or market investigator, and increasingly a technician, as more sophisticated products enter international trade.

Until fairly recently the main stream of business travel, particularly internationally, came from directors and top-ranking executives using first class. The trend has been, since the late fifties, for firms to adopt a tourist class policy for all but their very senior representatives. Whilst this has (in Europe, at least) caused some stagnation in the first class market, it has also led to a tendency for more and more relatively junior people to move on business. The fare may be higher, but the man is away for less time (so raising his productivity) and incurs less hotel expenses. Domestic and short international services have especially gained from this trend, and this particular market has a strong growth potential.

The same tendencies exist in the air cargo market which, compared with the over-all passenger air travel market, is in a much earlier stage of development. In contrast to the railways, air transport began with passengers and developed cargo carriage as a by-product in the relatively small baggage holds of passenger aircraft. Apart from the severe limitations hold size and hold-door size impose on the items of freight that can be carried in passenger aircraft, the costs of air transport, when reflected into cargo rates, are such that the great bulk of goods moving in international and domestic trade cannot afford them.

A manufacturer normally only extends his markets because he needs to do so. The tendency must always be to saturate the markets of easy access (usually those nearest to the factory) before facing the costs of selling further afield. Where price differentials can be secured that more than compensate for the costs of selling in different markets, then of course this will be another motive for going further afield. Much the same applies when 'further afield' implies exporting instead of selling on a home market. But, whatever the motivation, the manufacturer will not involve himself in higher distribution costs than are necessary.

The air transport marketing implications of the generally higher level of air cargo rates compared with surface cargo rates will be developed in a later chapter. For the purpose of this chapter it is only necessary to infer, from what has been said so far, that the higher the value of the goods in relative terms (e.g. value per pound weight) the more they are able to tolerate high carriage rates in return for other advantages such as speed, reduced danger of pilferage, etc.

As countries develop through their own particular industrial revolutions and beyond, it is typical of their products that the value per pound of weight increases. So that, both domestically and internationally, in addition to the traditional bulk movements of raw materials and basic food stuffs, trade widens to embrace surgical instruments, electrical apparatus and an ever-increasing range of items with a high absolute and relative value.

Already, at this end of the spectrum, air penetration of the total cargo market is considerable in some markets.

Other developments in air cargo have come about simply from the availability of markets by air that are not available by surface, the obvious examples being perishable goods and, in particular, cut flowers.

Although noticeable percentages of the items for which air transport offers particular advantages are already moving by air, these do represent the main growth points in international trade. Moreover, the percentage moving by surface is in many cases still quite considerable. In the circumstances, and particularly having regard to the fact that *generally* air cargo facilities, services and charges are much less highly developed than those for passengers, the potential for expansion of the air cargo market is very great.

It is indicative of the problems of providing an economically viable cargo service that there are few specialised freight aircraft in production, and only a handful of all-cargo air operators. Not the least of the difficulties is the one-way nature of cargo movement, so that a service which is to load well must find outward freight able to pay air rates and, separately, inward freight also in the high value category. And regular air cargo does not necessarily offer itself in such neatly reciprocal high-value streams.

However, the use of hold-space in passenger aircraft, reinforced by freighter conversions of passenger aircraft (including, in short-haul conditions, *ad hoc* conversions of aircraft carrying passengers by day and cargo by night), for all the limitations this imposes in size of consignment, has produced results. True freighters, built for the job, usually with swing-nose or swing-tail characteristics and special fittings, all designed to maximise consignment size and facilitate terminal handling, are increasingly seen on the world's air routes.

But it is difficult to make all-freighters pay even today, which is why their introduction is slow and somewhat tentative. However, this aspect of civil aviation is undoubtedly a major growth point. The airline know-how which went in the earlier years into the development of the passenger market is increasingly being turned on to cargo.

There is often talk of a 'break-through', imminent or incipient, in air cargo. The probability is that nothing quite so dramatic will be apparent. However, the barriers to development of this market are being eroded, and the sixties have seen the first real attempts to tackle the basic problems of cost.

There are undoubtedly considerable areas of cost reduction open, given an investment in specialised aircraft and terminal equipment. But, where an existing flow has been built up and is being met by a converted passenger aircraft (say, a Viscount, capacity 6 tons) the change even to a small specialised freighter (say, an Argosy, $10\frac{1}{2}$ tons) calls for an upward surge in traffic that is unattainable in the short term. This means that heavy investment in large specialised freighters, with attendant equipment and facilities, is unlikely to be remunerated immediately, or even proximately. Since the airline business on the whole is chronically on a knife-edge of profitability, boldness in air cargo development is noticeably lacking. Nevertheless, most major airlines are moving in this direction and the market, in regional and over-all terms, is certainly ripe for major expansion.

The market for mail develops, of course, with growth of population, the spread of literacy and wealth. It is very special, however, in that it develops in accordance with decisions made by a limited number of customers—the world's postal administrations.

The pricing of air mail will be dealt with in Chapter VI. But it will be obvious from the previous paragraph that, so long as *any* mail moves by surface, a decision by a postal administration to change the method of conveyance (as, for example, when the British postal administration decided to commence sending European mail (1936) and Empire mail (1937) by air at the same rate of postage as had previously applied to surface mail), can immediately expand the market enormously.

SOURCES USED IN THIS CHAPTER

International Civil Aviation Organisation Traffic Digests of Statistics and News Releases.
International Civil Aviation Organisation Annual Report of the Council to the Assembly for 1963.
American Aviation 15th Annual Air Transport Progress Review.
Air Transportation Association statement of progress of the industry in 1964.
'The progress of European Air Transport 1946–61', lecture by Lord Douglas of Kirtleside to the Royal Aeronautical Society, Nov. 1961.
Monthly Digest of Statistics (H.M. Stationery Office).
Appropriate Airline Annual Reports and Accounts.

CHAPTER V

MARKET RESEARCH

Generalities of the kind developed in the previous chapter may whet the appetite at the thought of the traffic available, but are of no assistance whatsoever in deciding what kind of air service to mount and between what points.

It is the job of market research to discover all that can be discovered (within the budget available!) about the requirements of the existing and potential customers for the air service. Its task is not merely to extrapolate trends and indicate that traffic between any two points will increase by x per cent over the planning period. It must also produce the kind of information which enables the type and style of the air service to be shaped to meet changing customer requirements as they arise, or preferably *before* they arise; in other words to steer the airlines into the kind of product development which is typical of all successful businesses.

Reading this kind of dynamism into what follows, the broad sweep of the market research task is directed towards the fulfilment of five distinct, though related, functions:

(*a*) To provide a detailed projection of demand by class, route, type of service, etc., to enable timetables to be constructed in time for the services to be on sale. This is normally a bi-annual (winter and summer) task, and involves, in the case of a large airline, beginning almost a year in advance of the introduction of each season's programme.

(*b*) To project demand in sufficient detail even further forward, perhaps up to five years or occasionally more, for specific purposes, in order that sensible decisions can be taken in respect of:

(i) Type, size and numbers of aircraft required at points in the future;
(ii) Ground facilities, including buildings and airports;
(iii) Over-all capital requirements;
(iv) Recruitment of staff (and provision of buildings to house

D

them), particularly staff requiring long periods of training, such as pilots.

(c) By derivation from (a) and (b) and similar projections of expected revenue rates, short and long term revenue forecasts must be produced, which can be set against cost forecasts for management control and budgetary purposes. Traffic and price forecasting must, of course, go hand in hand, since traffic volume will depend, *inter alia*, on price.

(d) To provide a break-down of forecasts into regional and other divisions necessary to indicate:

(i) Where the demand will arise (for example, all London–New York passengers do not buy their tickets in London);

(ii) What types of traffic, in what proportions, will make up total demand (first and tourist class, business, holiday, etc).

All this is designed to ensure that promotional efforts may be applied with the maximum of efficiency and economy.

(e) To monitor results and provide a feed-back so that future production and marketing plans may be modified.

As in any industry, serious error in forecasting can bring either disaster, because production costs are geared to a revenue which does not eventuate, or sales frustration because production quantities are set below actual demand. The burden on the airline forecaster is, however, particularly heavy.

In the short term, in order that production schedules can be set up, he has to forecast demand for a very wide range of products in detail and by period.

An airline timetable is a catalogue of numerous quite different *basic* products—the services between the different pairs of points on the network. These will run into some hundreds in the case of a major airline. Moreover, as outlined in Chapter II, production is specific to the day and time chosen for operation, so that even the same basic product—say a seat between London and Paris—has to be supplied in the hope and belief that at that time and on that day there will be a demand for it.

The forecast on which the timetable is set must, therefore, take into account, for each pair of points:

(a) Total demand during the period of the forecast;

(b) The way this demand will vary broadly through the period. For example, on a European holiday route demand in summer will be heaviest in July and August and taper away either side, with another peak at Easter (if this happens to fall in April; if it falls in March it is in the winter period);

(*c*) Detailed day of the week variations; the weekend being more popular for holiday routes but less popular for business routes;

(*d*) Attractiveness of different timings during the day;

(*e*) Effect on the basic demand pattern of the price structure.

The important point is that, for marketing purposes, the timetable must have integrity. Should the forecast be wrong, in that demand for one route is below expectation and demand for another above it, it may be technically feasible to switch aircraft, etc., from one to the other. This means cancelling a frequency on the disappointing route. Apart from the fact that *some* people will be booked on it, and their planned travel arrangements will be upset, there may be a repercussive effect on another route built into the original aircraft operating integrations.

The need to operate aircraft and crews as intensively as possible, because of the high cost of owning the former and employing the latter, means that any timetable, in peak seasons particularly, represents a closely knit integration with little to spare above the minimum necessary for maintenance and stand-by (reserves to meet last minute unserviceability and sickness).

Everything, therefore, militates against the correction of scheduling errors, due to faulty forecasting, during the currency of a published timetable, even by the holding of spare aircraft and crews which can correct under-production but not over-production.

An obvious corollary of this situation is that there is some sense in the forecaster erring on the side of caution, as at least this minimises the risks of financial loss to the enterprise. But, carried to extremes, this implies under-supply for almost all points and occasions, and this is no way to win friends, develop markets and gain operating licences from the authorities. Essentially, the basis of the forecast should be clearly stated and, if possible, the changes that would result if any of the assumptions were changed should be calculated.

It is impossible in one brief chapter to outline a course in airline market research as used for traffic forecasting. The following, therefore, is intended as no more than a generalised description of the *kind* of factors that will be taken into account.

Example A: An existing route, operated in the similar season last year and probably also in previous years.

In assessing likely demand in the scheduling period due for settlement, the forecaster will start with the following historic data as *facts:*

(*a*) Demand in the most recent similar period, broken down into (*b*) Month (or part month if appropriate), day of week, day and night and, in specific cases, time of day down to the hour:

(*c*) If he is fortunate, *some* less detailed information about carrying by other transport operators—air, rail, sea, road—between the same points:

(*d*) Trend lines of growth (or decline) leading up to all the latest figures:

(*e*) Specific events in the past which can be seen, in retrospect, to have affected development (for example, aircraft type change, new competitors, fare changes, etc.).

In deciding, on the basis of all this data, how he should extrapolate the historic trends for his own airline, the following will be pertinent questions[1] to which answers must be given:

(*a*) What special factors will influence over-all demand (incidence of Easter, Olympic Games, National Fairs, etc.)?

(*b*) Is the airline's own product going to be better (new aircraft, improved frequency), worse, or much the same?

(*c*) The same question in respect of the direct competition (that is, other transport operations between the same points), absolutely and relatively.

(*d*) Is there likelihood of change in the interline situation, that is, in the pattern of operations of other airlines who historically have fed traffic on to, or taken onward traffic from, the route under review?

(*e*) Will the fares and rates for the airline and for the competition be the same, rise or fall?

(*f*) What is the quantitative assessment of the competition's and the airline's own potential?

(*g*) What indications are there of the trend of general economic activity in the selling areas feeding the route and so affecting purchasing ability (forecasts of gross national product, disposable income, hire purchase and bank loan developments, etc.)?

(*h*) Similar considerations affecting the political situation (for example, elections) and in this case the reception end is of even more importance (unsettled political conditions getting worse or better).

(*i*) In regard to holiday traffic, what is the trend of the price and availability of accommodation (hotels, villas, etc.), particularly in relation to other holiday areas, since holiday-makers are concerned with their *total* holiday cost?

Example B: A new route.

In this case the forecast is designed primarily to decide whether the

---

[1] The most difficult task in market research is to ask the right questions. If one can do this, the questions themselves infer what must be done to find the right answers.

new route should be opened at all, and secondarily to settle the capacity to be offered.

Much the same processes as in Example A will need to be worked through, but absence of the data which can only be obtained by experience will be overcome in various ways, for example:

(a) There may well be some existing surface and air connections, even indirect, and sometimes traffic by these can be discovered or broadly calculated to give some idea of potential:

(b) Tourist statistics by nationality of visitors, issued by most countries, can also indicate potential:

(c) In a limited number of cases actual visas, issued at the reception end to nationals of the State from which the air service starts, are obtainable and give a very fair idea of existing movement:

(d) In the case of new domestic routes, a few quite simple statistics shown by experience to correlate broadly with travel, when compared with the same statistics for a point already served, can give a very clear indication of potential. Such key statistics are population (over eighteen years of age is better), number of inhabitants or families with incomes above a level set by experience of the particular national market, number of domestic telephones, telephone call traffic and car registrations.

The amalgam of these varied and detailed forecasts will demonstrate the shape of the desirable programme of services to be offered, desirable in the sense that, given a reasonably accurate set of forecasts, production can be organised to meet it within such limitations as are imposed by physical and financial factors. This process of meshing in the commercial requirement with production possibilities is the subject of Chapter VIII.

Staying with short term forecasting, the traffic estimates which have been used to plan the programme are used simultaneously for the production of revenue forecasts for management control purposes.

Within the marketing department these revenue forecasts are also used for sales control purposes. The over-all revenue forecast will not only consist of all the money earned on all the routes, but can also be totalled by adding up the forecast sales in all markets—the two totals are, of course, the same.

The marketing director and his management staff not only need to know what revenue a particular route or service earns in total, but *where* the actual sales are made. The sales on an international service starting from London, New York or Sydney will be effected, at least, all over Great Britain, the USA and Australia respectively. The same will be true of travel from the other terminal point or points of these services. In addition, a larger or smaller percentage of each, dependent on circumstances, will be sold off-line: for example, London–New York sold in Copenhagen, Sydney–Tokyo sold in Auckland. Furthermore, the home market of an airline, its base of operations, will be selling directly many services, while a peripheral point on its network will only *directly* be selling one.

The historic scatter of these sales can be known by analysis of collected passenger tickets, all of which show place of issue, or from the comparable freight documentation. This detailed information will be used as a guide to breaking down the *future* revenue targets of the various sales areas. The detail in which this is done will be entirely a matter of management decision, an important element in this decision being the very substantial cost of such analyses and the staff time necessary to make effective use of them. But, unless this sales distribution is plotted in some detail, the marketing organisation cannot be intelligently shaped, nor can its detailed effectiveness be measured.

Within each market, the actual volume of sales having been determined by methods such as those described, research will also be needed to determine characteristics. Such subdivisions as income level, age and sex distribution, nature of business and industrial activity, will have to be discovered in order to guide advertising and other promotional activity.

To summarise, the market research section, in its short term forecasting capacity, produces traffic estimates on which operating programmes are based and from which are calculated revenue forecasts for over-all management purposes, as well as sales targets to guide promotional effort. All this may be regarded as the tactical aspect of market research.

The strategic element in forecasting comes in when the forward estimating of traffic is used for planning future resources, and not the use of existing resources. And this kind of long term forecasting is essentially designed to aid management decisions in respect of numbers, types and sizes of aircraft.

In almost no conditions can an airline order at short notice a modern aircraft 'off the peg'. In fact new aircraft that are available immediately are probably those that are not selling. A successful aircraft will be coming off the production line to meet orders accepted in rotation, which may well have been placed a year or more ago. With a new type, the manufacturer will seek to interest potential customers at the design stage, and will hope to take orders at this point. Where, as has been typical of the British Corporations, they work with the manufacturers from a specification put up by the airline, the forecasting necessary to any kind of intelligent specification will stretch forward at least five years.

Forecasts for this purpose will not be in such detail as for programme planning. They must, however, be grouped in such a way as to give indications of range and size. An airline with routes varying from 2000 miles to 200 miles would not order one fleet type capable of the longer range, intending to use it everywhere. Severe economic penalties arise if a longer range aircraft is used for the shorter ranges; on the other hand, there are considerable economies in limiting the number of different types in a fleet. The choice of the ideal fleet composition for a particular route pattern is, therefore, a compromise, and the traffic forecasts enabling this choice to be made must be in route, or grouped route, detail.

The question of size is particularly difficult. In general, the larger the aircraft, the higher the aircraft-mile costs but the lower the seat-mile or capacity-ton-mile costs. A very large aircraft, deployed on a route with little traffic offering, will lose all the advantage of its low capacity unit costs if a small aircraft, with lower aircraft-mile costs, could carry the load. Even if all the load could be economically accommodated by operating at very low frequency, this in itself would discourage traffic, particularly if competitive operators with smaller aircraft offer higher frequency.

So forecasts for this purpose, within the grouped route estimates, must assess broad patterns of demand at peak and trough periods. These forecasts must be read in conjunction with a view as to the size of aircraft likely to be used at the operative time by other airlines involved in the route pattern. From this a calculation has to be made of desirable frequency, both at peak and trough, and at this point an idea of the size of aircraft most likely to suit the market requirement will emerge. For similar reasons, the type of aircraft to be ordered must be decided against an assessment of the competition's known or assumed plans, and this aspect offers its own acute brand of headache at times of dramatic technical innovations (prop-jet, pure jet, supersonic).

Within the general task of forecasting for production and capital planning and sales control purposes, many lines of enquiry will be brought together—population and income trends, competitors' known plans (for example, announced aircraft orders), customer response to particular aspects of the airline's 'product range' and so forth. But the market research section should also be pursuing, independently of the forecasting function, projects designed to assist management decision in developing the services offered by the airline.

Product testing is not particularly easy for air transport, as *measurable* differences between a set standard (or the standard set by the competition) and the achieved standards are only possible within a limited field.

Punctuality and regularity are two obvious aspects where measurement is possible. Less obvious aspects which are capable of measurement are average delays in dealing with telephone enquiries and re-servations, time taken for baggage clearance and other functions of passenger handling.

These objective methods of measurement may either be organised by the market research section or by the departments responsible for the particular functions. The results, however, should all be made available to market research as, together with such similar informa-tion as can be gathered about the competition, and even in isolation in so far as the measurements change over time, they will have an effect on judgment of market shares.

Next there is the whole field of consumer research. A method of testing customer satisfaction is the 'in-flight' survey. All passengers on a particular service are asked to complete a questionnaire, carefully compiled to produce answers which can be analysed statistically, either to give a general view of what the customers do or do not like about the service provided, or to test out in more detail passenger reactions to a specific aspect, particularly perhaps an innovation. There is a tendency for market research men to want to operate in-flight surveys fairly frequently in their pursuit of knowledge, and for the promotional side to object because of the irritating effect on regular passengers.

But, useful as such techniques may be, designed to analyse the likes and dislikes of existing passengers, the questions one really wants to ask are aimed at the people who are *not* travelling. Here, apart from any analysis that may be possible of the negative responses received by the sales staff who are doing leg-work in pursuit of business, the only device is basically the door-knocker survey. For this it is essential to employ one of the specialist firms in the field, and it will always be expensive; therefore, it can only be used occasionally. It is particularly important that the information required should be very carefully thought out and explained to the firm undertaking the work.

Finally, there is the important task of analysing the historic results of innovation and advising on the probable results of projects under discussion. This nearly always relates to tariff changes. Historic as-sessment of this kind is much more difficult than it seems, for in re-viewing past results there are always several factors which have affected the trend, in addition to the particular change which is to be assessed. Nevertheless, unless assessments of this kind are regularly attempted, tariffs policy has no sound foundation on which to develop.

CHAPTER VI

PRICING

The use of price flexibility as a marketing tool in air transport is limited by both economic and regulatory considerations. In Chapter II the basic reasons why air transport prices (fares and rates) can, and indeed should, vary other than over time, were outlined. The external controls on the freedom of the individual operator to vary his tariff were, in turn, described in Chapter III.

In devising a pricing policy, although average costs may have little influence in the fixing of individual fares or rates, the actual tariff that emerges to deal with the problem of demand variations, should be constructed with the elements that go to make up total costs very much in mind.

Basically the situation is that an airline's costs break down into those which are escapable in the short term, the intermediate term, and the long term. These can be called, in the same order, direct, allocated and overhead costs.

If an aeroplane flies between two places, the direct costs involved are fuel and oil, landing fees, those engineering costs which are related precisely to hours flown, and other variables such as passenger meals. All these are costs which simply are not incurred at all if a particular flight does not take place.

On the other hand, if a decision is taken not to operate a flight, the cost of owning the aeroplane (capital charges, amortisation and insurance), employing the crew and running the terminal services will go on. Most of these costs can be switched away from one route to another, re-allocated, at relatively short notice. In practice, however, the notice is not so short, because of the necessity of maintaining timetable integrity. Terminal staff and installations, in any case, are only mobile on a planned basis. The airline that has its traffic staff, station engineers, tractors and so on panicking round the routes on a day to day basis would spend a lot of money *and* lose its best station staff.

Nevertheless, all these costs, once an operation has been set up, can be regarded as allocated to the particular operation with varying degrees of precision and, on a seasonal basis at least, can be re-deployed to other work if there is a shift in demand.

Meanwhile, the overhead, the true long term cost, goes on whether the airline flies or does not fly. Such costs—the head office organisation, base engineering, even much of the sales and advertising effort—cannot be allocated with any precision to particular operations, nor can it be adjusted over-all except in the long run.

Using the British European Airways figures (1963–64) as an example, because they are published in appropriate detail, Table 4 gives the percentage break-down of total costs on the basis set out above.[1]

TABLE 4. *Break-down of BEA's total costs for 1963–64*

Direct	34%
Allocated	43%
Overhead	23%

These percentages will not necessarily be the same for other airlines, nor will each route have exactly the same cost considerations. The argument is not affected by such differences, as they will not change the approximate weight of the separate broad items of cost in each particular instance.

Assuming for ease of exposition that one is examining the fare structure for a purely passenger route, the aim, of course, will be to ensure that total revenue covers total costs in the period for which the fare structure is being set. Although one may do shorter period calculations for specific purposes, the fares should be set for their effect on a year's results because accounting periods, on which profit and loss judgments are made, usually cover the full year,

Of course, a particular flight may operate with such a small load that direct costs are not covered, but fares have to be judged on their over-all effect during the period for which they operate, rather than from flight to flight.

Taking all the routes in an airline's network, and using the BEA figures quoted in Table 4, the first requirement is that *each* covers its direct and allocated costs. All the routes between them will then cover 77 per cent of total costs. Provided that between them they also cover the 23 per cent of overhead, all is well. The division of the overhead between routes on some average formula is quite artificial. There is no logical reason at all why one route should not, if it can,

---

[1] The grouping used to calculate these percentages is slightly different from that in App. 5 to the BEA Report and Accounts; for tariff considerations my grouping is more useful and this implies treating commission as a deduction from revenue rather than a variable cost, and engineering base and advertising as overhead rather than allocated costs.

bear a heavier proportion of the overheads (that is, show a larger surplus over variables plus allocated costs) than another.

If, in spite of fare adjustments and changed operating patterns, a particular route does not even cover the 77 per cent, then resources are being wastefully allocated and should be re-deployed. If there is no way of re-deploying to achieve the desired result, the airline should probably contract, selling equipment and running down staff, if it wants to stay solvent. All this assumes that any period of acceptable loss in launching a new service has passed and that future promise of improvement is too speculative or distant to be economically justifiable.

Looking further into the detail of a particular route which is, over the year, covering at least its 77 per cent, again it is unimportant if at certain periods it contributes more or less than this on average, provided that there is no time when it consistently earns less than the 34 per cent represented by direct costs. If this is happening, every such flight is literally costing more in short term outgoings than it is taking in as revenue.

Of course, no airline is run with such perfection and minute cost introspection as this picture would imply, and all manner of considerations may cause managements (usually for relatively short periods only) to turn a blind eye to economics. The commercial airline must, however, operate within the limits set by its own cost composition. And, for the purposes of this chapter, these relatively simplified arguments are sufficient to demonstrate the wide limits within which an economically sound differential fares structure can operate.

Furthermore, even though a service, or all the services together, may be economic on the most careful examination of costs on the lines described here, it may still be possible to improve the position of the route or the whole network by fares adjustments.

In an endeavour to bring this somewhat theoretical defence of the differential fares system to life, the following arithmetical example, falling within the limits set by the percentages used in Table 4, may demonstrate more clearly the value of a flexible approach to pricing.

For a given route the average costs of operating a 100 seat aircraft, including full contribution to overheads, is £1,000 for the round trip. Using the percentages derived from the BEA accounts this implies £340 direct costs, £430 allocated costs and £230 contribution to overheads. If the fare were set at £20 return, this would require an average load factor of only 50 per cent to break even.

If this is a European holiday route and the schedule consists of a daily return flight completed between 1000 hours and 2000 hours, with a nightly return flight completed between 2200 hours and 0800 hours, passenger preference on a fare of £20 might well produce a weekly traffic pattern as in Table 5.

TABLE 5. *Example of traffic pattern resulting from standard fare*

		£
Day flights:	Friday, Saturday and Sunday, 70% load factor, revenue £1,400 per flight. Total revenue (3 flights)	4,200
Night flights:	Friday, Saturday and Sunday, 60% load factor, revenue £1,200 per flight. Total revenue (3 flights)	3,600
Day flights:	Monday, Tuesday, Wednesday, Thursday, 40% load factor, revenue £800 per flight. Total revenue (4 flights)	3,200
Night flights:	Monday, Tuesday, Wednesday, Thursday, 20% load factor, revenue £400 per flight. Total revenue (4 flights)	1,600
	Total revenue (14 flights)	12,600

This route is meeting exactly 90 per cent of its total costs, thus answering our requirement of variables plus allocated costs (77 per cent) and something quite substantial towards overheads. Moreover, even the night mid-week services are covering 40 per cent of total costs, well in excess of variables (34 per cent).

On the face of it, and if all routes together are covering total costs, this is a perfectly satisfactory state of affairs. However, introduction of a system of differential fares might have the results illustrated in Table 6.

TABLE 6. *Example of traffic pattern resulting from differential fares*

		£
Day weekend:	fare £20, 60% load factor, revenue £1,200 per flight. Total revenue (3 flights)	3,600
Night weekend:	fare £16, 80% load factor, revenue £1,280 per flight. Total revenue (3 flights)	3,840
Day mid-week:	fare £16, 60% load factor, revenue £960 per flight. Total revenue (4 flights)	3,840
Night mid-week:	fare £12, 80% load factor, revenue £960 per flight. Total revenue (4 flights)	3,840
	Total revenue (14 flights)	15,120

The route is now producing a weekly profit of £1,120 on *total* costs, and yet no fare has been raised, and most have been lowered. In fact, on these figures there is a chance that lowering the day week-end fare would produce a higher revenue on those services than the £20 fare. If it is reduced too much, however, the traffic may not be available for the other, lower-priced days and timings, so upsetting the profitable balance.

Whilst it is true that the load factors in this example have (of course!) been carefully worked out to produce the desired result, they are not unrealistic and the example does demonstrate clearly the use of a flexible pricing policy as a marketing tool.

The whole process depends on the elasticity of demand. Lower fares for off-peak times, days and seasons will generally attract new traffic, as well as tend to re-distribute it somewhat more conveniently for the airline. If the effect of a lower fare is to attract so little new traffic that the total revenue is less than at the higher fare, then demand is inelastic and the reduction was a mistake. On a mixed business and holiday route in summer, it may pay to have a fare structure of the kind shown in Table 6.

Another, and perhaps more universal device, is a set of lower fares in what are called 'shoulder' months. In Northern European conditions the peak holiday period is mid-June until towards the end of September, the shoulder months then being April to mid-June and October. Again, elasticity of demand is probably positive and the total revenue is increased by the lower fares. But in the true off-peak for holiday travel it may well be that demand is inelastic; fare reductions will not attract sufficient new traffic to compensate for the general lowering of the revenue rate on the traffic which, for its own reasons, will be travelling in the trough period in any case. For this reason, fares at times of lowest demand may actually be at the highest level for the route.

The result of all this is that, internationally and domestically, air-lines have a basic pattern of fares, single and return, for such classes as they operate (for example, first and tourist). In addition they pro-bably have a series of creative fares, almost always for return trips only, and only exceptionally applicable to first class travel. These creative fares are those that result from the inherent flexibility in the pricing process, and are the price-inducement instruments available to the marketing side.

The approach to cargo rating is fundamentally different, though the object is the same; namely to devise a tariff with the end object of filling the aeroplanes and covering costs. The difference lies in the well known phrase which describes transport cargo rating: 'charging what the traffic will bear'. All this means is that there is a low rate for, say, coal and a high rate for gold. The shipper has no choice. The equivalent approach, if applied to passenger transport, would be to charge people according to some kind of means test. In fact the passenger fares approach is to fix fares which anybody can use if they choose to meet the conditions, whereas gold simply cannot masquerade as coal.

Broadly the international air cargo rating system throughout the world has the following characteristics:

(a) A basic rate between each pair of points expressed per pound or per kilogram which will apply to *any* cargo. The tendency is for these rates to be less per mile over longer distances, because much of the cost of carrying cargo is in the handling at either end, which is constant irrespective of the distance.

(*b*) A multitude of 'commodity rates', aimed at attracting particular flows of traffic which cannot bear the basic rate. These may be narrowly specified as to route and commodity, or broader, embracing a group of commodities (e.g. textiles) and a related set of routes (e.g. across the North Atlantic).

(*c*) Rebates for both (*a*) and (*b*) when the consignment reaches a certain size (e.g. 45 kgs.) because some terminal costs—documentation, accounting, etc.—are the same for all consignments. There may be several such rate reduction 'break-points' (e.g. 45; 250; and 500 kgs.)

(*d*) Minimum charges—usually set quite high—because of the heavy incidence of terminal handling and documentation costs.

(*e*) A 'volumetric' surcharge, to ensure that very light but bulky cargoes pay for the space they take up in the aircraft.

(*f*) A 'value' surcharge, so that exceptionally high value cargo, such as gold, pays what it really can bear!

From the airline marketing man's point of view, the only interesting aspect is the commodity rate. Because so much cargo is still carried on passenger aircraft, and available cargo space in such cases will vary enormously with frequency and aircraft type, formulae of the kind developed for passenger fares have no place. In the end the rate is a matter of negotiation between potential shippers and airlines, and the actual levels will depend on the widely divergent circumstances of individual cases.

As specialist cargo aircraft are introduced, a closer look is necessary at the effects of the cargo rating system inherited from the mixed passenger–cargo days. Even so, cargo between any two points served by the typical 'mainly passenger' airline will move either solely in passenger aircraft or in passenger aircraft *and* pure freighters. Only very exceptionally does a cargo-flow move exclusively in freighters. In developing cargo traffic, it is true that the passenger and freighter aircraft on the same route support each other. It is also true that it is very difficult to cost out in practically useful terms the carriage of cargo on passenger aircraft, unless it can be shown that passenger load is regularly displaced by a cargo traffic flow.

So for marketing purposes, one must be satisfied by saying there is considerable latitude available to the average airline in varying its rates to attract particular cargo traffic flows; that the limits will be quite peculiar to each airline, and within each airline to its individual routes; and that the present very diffuse pattern that emerges from

63

this situation will eventually crystallise into something more closely limited by cost break-down considerations as pure freighters dominate the air cargo market. But that is very much in the future.

So much (or so little) for the economic limitations on differential pricing. But what about the regulatory shackles which keep individual airline's pricing from roaming at will within these limitations?

Internationally, the effective control on an airline's pricing freedom is exercised through the IATA Traffic Conference machinery, behind which lie Government sanctions as described in Chapter III.

An international airline, having decided on the pattern of fares and rates it wants, takes these to the Traffic Conference appropriate to its area of operation. These Conferences meet every two years, usually all together. It is possible, but not too easy, to effect changes in basic rates and fares between Conferences by Mail Vote. Similarly, if major economic changes due to such factors as inflation are occurring in an area, special Conferences may be called. Creative fares and commodity rates, on the other hand, cannot be fixed for such long periods, if only because they are designed to meet changing market situations. Boards specially constituted for the purpose meet not infrequently, therefore, between Conferences, to agree new creative fares or commodity rates and cancel or vary those that exist. Mail Vote procedures are also used for the same purpose, particularly in the case of commodity rates.

In all cases unanimity is necessary and it may well be asked how this is possible, with so many airlines all probably requiring incompatible fares and rates because of differing economic or other circumstances.

The first thing to be said is that securing a set of fares or rates based on a new marketing philosophy is certainly not easy. Securing a fare or rate between points which have not had that *type* of rate or fare previously, but which is in line with an accepted and existing pattern, is much less of a problem.

Every airline, from the largest to the smallest, starts with the weakness inherent in having to ensure that not one negative vote remains against any of its proposals if they are to go through. It also, however, has the strength of knowing that other airlines' proposals cannot succeed against *its* negative votes. The result is, in effect, a multi-lateral negotiation with compromises, of necessity, being made, leading in the end to all the fares and rates and their related conditions being voted in without any negatives. The package may not contain all that a particular airline sought from the Conference. Nevertheless, if its arguments are sound and the airline is seeking reductions, the final result is almost certainly going to trend in the direction it wants. In the event of complete break-down, Governments have to fix the fares and rates. They may merely re-validate the *status quo* until all the airlines can agree on changes. But a strong Government may step in and support, with other Governments, the line its airline unsuccessfully followed. The lower fares that were introduced on the North Atlantic in summer 1963 derived from just such a set of circumstances.

To summarise, although the regulatory machinery for setting international fares and rates offers the airline many problems in securing the price structure it requires, it does not work to protect the inefficient or timid who require high fares and are scared of experiment. It does resolve genuine clashes of interest and philosophy between the efficient. And, once the structure has been agreed, it leaves the airline free to concentrate on marketing planning, knowing that unheralded price changes in the scheduled air transport field in which it operates will not occur.

Regulation of domestic and cabotage airline pricing varies, of course, from country to country. The typical situation, however, where control exists, is for a Government body to rule on the price level on cases made to it by the airlines. The position is in some ways similar to that which exists internationally. Instead of convincing all the other airlines in IATA, however, the airline requiring change has to convince the regulatory body, whose eventual ruling then offers stability as in the case of international fares and rates. But there is the fundamental difference that the airline is not negotiating, but pleading, and it has no powers of veto to help achieve its objective. But then, nor have any competitors who may object to the proposed fare change.

Mail pricing is quite different again. It is specifically excluded from the IATA price-making machinery and is normally also excluded from the competence of national regulatory bodies.

The postal administrations of the world are joined together in the Universal Postal Union. This is the body by virtue of whose agreements the whole movement of international mail takes place, including the 'knock-for-knock' aspect which is at the core of it and whereby a stamp, purchased from one national post office, will ensure the delivery of a letter in any other UPU State. The UPU also virtually fixes the rates which will be paid for the international carriage of mail by air.

The system works in this way. The postal administrations agree together in the UPU the rates they will pay each other for the *on-carriage* of mail, that is to say for mail handed by one postal administration to another for onward transmission to others. There are only two such rates, the higher for first class mail and the lower for other mail (including parcel post). So far as the airlines are concerned, this results in the national postal administration of any particular airline paying over to it the charges for *all* the international mail it carries, any settlements being effected between postal administrations. Thus it is likely that a carrier will receive the same basic rates for all the international mail it carries of the two categories, the actual rates it receives being the subject of negotiation between itself and its national postal administration.

The tendency, of course, must be for the level of rate received to be the same as the agreed U P U settlement rate. But it need not be. The postal administration could drive a hard bargain and refuse to pay as much. Similarly, if a Government wishes to subsidise its airline it can do so by paying a generous mail rate.

Cabotage mail rates are entirely a matter of negotiation between an airline and its postal authorities. Here again the actual rates vary from the closest of commercial bargains to very high rates deliberately designed to provide a subsidy.

Reverting to the question of passenger fares, it is worth examining in a little detail some of the different *kinds* of fares which have emerged within the concept of differential fares.

The basic, or standard, fare for each class will be the highest. Traditionally, nearly all forms of transport have given a reduction for a return ticket—that is to say, the out and back journeys could be purchased for less than twice the single fare. From the carrier's point of view, this had three main objects or advantages:

(*a*) It committed the passenger, to a greater or lesser extent, to returning by the same carrier;

(*b*) The carrier had cash in hand earlier than would otherwise be the case;

(*c*) Some slight reductions in cost might arise on ticket issue and reservations.

However, there are penalties. All tariffs must be published with single and return fares shown, and inter-company accounting for interline business is considerably complicated. On the whole, the trend is away from this discount. The formula for international air journeys until 1963 was to give a 10 per cent reduction for a return ticket: that is, the round trip fare was 180 per cent of the single fare. Since 1963 it has been 5 per cent (round trip 190 per cent of single). Domestically many instances can be found (of which the United Kingdom is one) where the discount has been eliminated entirely, the return ticket costing the sum of two single tickets.

Unfortunately, action on changes of this kind must always be seen in relation to the effect on fare levels as a whole. One cannot eliminate the round trip discount without changing some fares up or down. The simplest (and normal) cases consist of keeping the single fares where they are, so raising return fares, or retaining return fares and thus reducing single fares.

E

Some airline marketing men would be sorry to see the discount go. They feel it does hold some return traffic to the airline issuing the ticket, in spite of the ease in transferring to another airline, or returning by surface and claiming a refund of the difference between the single and return fares. Finance departments of some airlines like the 'money in advance' that the round trip discount gives them; others believe the really large administrative costs that would be saved in interline accounting, if the discount disappeared, would more than off-set this. In the end, the probability is that the discount will disappear as a relatively painless way of raising fares (by making all return fares double the existing single fares) at a time when rising costs call for higher fares.

The creative fares, that is those below the basic fares, introduced to promote extra traffic, all have some kind of restriction designed to make them unattractive to those already paying (and so willing and/ or able to continue to pay) the basic fare. Apart from limitations in applicability to periods, day of the week, etc., as already described, the following are typical restrictions:

(a) Making all such fares return fares. There is a not inconsiderable amount of traffic which travels at single fares of necessity, and this would be true particularly in cases of journeys which are not of a simple out and back nature. By making all cheap fares available only for a return journey between any two points, all single journey and multisector traffic is automatically excluded and pays the higher fare.

(b) Making excursion fares purchasable only in the country of origin. This is the most important feature so far as international creative fares are concerned. One of the basic aspects of the IATA tariff-making machinery is that the final result is a completely integrated set of world-wide fares. Through fares between points all over the world are either specified or constructed by the use of existing fares, and the whole structure is so designed that it is impossible to purchase two sector fares, making up the through fare, in such a way that the total price paid undercuts the through fare.

Creative fares are introduced to develop particular markets and the object is not to dilute other revenue. If it were possible to add a creative fare from, say, London to a point in Europe, to a fare from North America to London, this would probably undercut the through fare from New York to the point in Europe. As the whole object of the fare structure is to aim it at the traffic flows concerned, in the way that has been described, the creative fares between London and European points are sold only in the United Kingdom, and thus avoid the dilution inherent in tacking them on to the end of through fares.

(c) Limited validity. The normal validity of the standard fares is for one year. The traditional method of limiting dilution by creative fares is to limit their validity—either to fourteen days, twenty-one days or at the most one month. This is not a very satisfactory method as the bulk of the traffic which is liable to dilution from cheaper fares is business traffic which, on the whole, does not tend to go away for simple return journeys for periods longer than a month.

(d) Minimum stay. This is the reverse of (c) and much more effective. In effect, as the fare is beamed at the holiday-maker who is going away for a specific length of time on holiday, the rule may say that the return journey must not be undertaken less than, say, seven days from the date of the outward journey. This effectively stops dilution of revenue from business traffic on short visits. On the other hand, as soon as such a rule is introduced, any pleasure traffic of a weekend nature which might be developed by a cheap creative fare is automatically excluded.

(e) Group fares. These are cheaper fares available provided a group of a minimum number travel together. The numbers may be as small as fifteen or even go up to twenty-five, and are usually of this order. The problem here is to ensure that one is attracting a group, and not merely putting into the travel agents' hands the ability to take twenty bookings to the same place for people who happen to be travelling on the same day (and this would not be unrealistic in the case of a big agent) and call them a group, thus securing the reduction. If there were no safeguards they could go even further and attract this traffic in accordance with the group rule. A lot of effort has, therefore, gone into devising rules to ensure that the group starts off with having an affinity other than the desire to secure cheap travel! These rules cause a great deal of difficulty and trouble, and there is considerable difference of opinion amongst airline men as to whether such group fares really do achieve their objective. The airlines operating within Europe have not, on the whole, introduced such fares, believing that the other devices that they use are more effective and much more easily controlled.

(f) Family fares. This is a device whereby the first member of a family pays full fare and subsequent members pay less than the full fare. The object is either to persuade business men when travelling to take their wives with them, or to keep the fares high for holiday-makers travelling by themselves (single people who can probably afford the fare), and get the family business which may be less able to afford the higher fares. Such fares are common in North America, but again have not been introduced to any considerable degree in Europe. One of the reasons is that, certainly so far as traffic from the U K is concerned, any concession which makes family travel, as such, cheaper than individual travel, is liable merely to increase pressure at peak periods owing to the school holiday problem.

(g) Special fares or discounts for inclusive tours (packaged holi-days). These are made available solely to agents for constructing their all-inclusive holidays, in return for which they have to give evidence of offering a complete package and also of promoting it by means of printed literature etc. This type of fare is used a good deal in Europe, particularly for traffic from the United Kingdom to the Continent, and has been responsible for the great development of the packaged holiday traffic on the scheduled airlines. It is probably the least dilutionary of all the devices. The fares normally are only applicable to holiday places where business men do not go to the same extent, and the holidays constructed on them by the agents are usually of fixed duration and, consequently, would only exceptionally suit the requirements of a business man or the wealthier holiday maker.

All these tariff devices are, in effect, disadvantages which accompany cheaper fares. Any member of the public can take advantage of the appropriate fares if the particular limitation is acceptable. Neverthe-less, arguments do arise at times as to whether there is an element of discrimination inherent in the restrictions. This is important if the public feel that this is so, leading to resentment and bad public re-lations. Airlines, perhaps more than most organisations, do like to be loved, and are much more sensitive to general public criticism (how-ever ill-informed this may sometimes be) than their critics generally believe.

Discrimination is, however, much more important in societies which have carried a democratic sensitiveness on this point to the stage where legislative prohibition of such practices exists. The United States is a prime example of this. Special fares, available only to agents who use them to construct package holidays, though accepted throughout Europe, have not been acceptable on discrimination grounds by the Civil Aeronautics Board, the regulatory body in the United States for such matters.[1] Nevertheless, after great pressure by the airlines, the Civil Aeronautics Board did accept such tour-basing fares to operate on the North Atlantic in 1966.

In some parts of the world other fares of a more overtly discrimina-tory nature, in that they are only open to defined sections of the public, are sometimes found. These may be promotional, for example special fares for ships' crews, students or honeymoon couples; social (fares for the blind) or, in effect, political (reductions for mem-bers of the armed services and their dependants, civil servants, etc.).

When devising a promotional fares structure, however logical this may be, there are two general rules that should not be forgotten.

The first is not to allow tariff-making logic to outrage public logic.

[1] Tour Basing Fares 14 CAB 257 (1951).

It may be perfectly reasonable, on marketing grounds, to have a special promotional fare to a further point which is cheaper than the fare to a nearer point. But if the two points are both served by the same stopping service, the passenger with the cheap ticket to the further point has to be charged an excess fare if, discovering what he thinks is an anomaly, he gets off the aeroplane at the intermediate (dearer) point. The most elegant exposition of the theory of differential pricing in such cases will fail to convince the bewildered traveller that there is not a strong element of insanity in such a situation.

Cases of the kind mentioned are extreme; common sense and a feeling for public relations dictate that they should not be allowed to creep into the tariff. But even the normal differential fares have this danger to a slight extent. Any member of the public can realise from published information, that the single fare he is paying is only fractionally less than the return fare that the man sitting in the seat next to him may be paying. Fortunately, the general idea of 'excursion fares' has been inherent in surface transport for so long that people are conditioned to them, and complaints on this score are very few.

The second general rule is to avoid over-complication. In the end, the fares and rates structure is a price list of the services which are on sale. It fails in its purpose if it requires an abnormally high IQ to understand it. Logical tariff-making, for example, could call for a different fare for different timings through the day, on a high frequency service, in addition to seasonal, day of the week, and day and night variations. Apart from the burden on the prospective traveller of unravelling this particular piece of complexity, there is a real cost to the airline in the extended time each booking takes while the clerk himself (a) works out the right fare and (b) explains it to the client.

The fare structure to holiday resorts in Europe from Britain is often criticised as being too complicated. An extreme example is Palma, and the fare table to and from London in 1965–66 was as detailed in Table 7.

TABLE 7. *Fares London–Palma 1965–66*

LONDON–PALMA AND VICE VERSA

NORMAL FARES			CREATIVE FARES (TOURIST CLASS RETURN)			
	£	s	1 April–15 June and 1–31 Oct.		16 June– 30 Sept.	1 Nov.– 31 Mar.
First single	36	3				
First return	68	14				
Tourist single	26	0		£ s	£ s	£ s
Tourist return	49	8				
			Day weekend	36 18	44 8	—
			Day mid-week	36 18	36 18	—
			Night weekend	33 14	36 18	36 18
			Night mid-week	32 8	32 8	36 18

Validity 1 month

Night fares applicable to flights started and completed 2000–0800 hours.

This *is* complicated, but since it fulfils its purpose and leads to relatively few complaints, it cannot be regarded as *too* complex. In any case the British holiday-maker is now reasonably conditioned to a fare structure which gives cheaper fares for night and mid-week travel, and is also conditioned to high season charges being heavier than at other times (this being an old-established resort hotel practice) so that the variety of fares does not really act as a deterrent.

To conclude this chapter, it is worth considering the implications of the 'stand-by' fares introduced on certain of the domestic routes in the United Kingdom in April 1963, because these fares demonstrate clearly the problems of dilution.

An airline that sells 60 per cent or more of its total capacity on average throughout the year is doing well in matching scheduled services to the demand. The fact still remains that 40 per cent runs to waste. And, unlike unused machine time in a factory, the production in the case of an airline actually takes place. The empty seat moves with the full seat and the extra cost of having a passenger in it would be infinitesimal in relation to the fare. The whole tariff policy and the operating plan are designed to minimise this waste, but a great deal of capacity is still unfilled. Most airline men at some time or another speculate on the possibility of finding a philosopher's stone which will transmute those empty passenger seats into gold.

The obvious course to follow is to maintain the existing structure, with confirmed bookings for each seat sold, and encourage people who cannot afford the published fares to come to the airport and 'stand by', ready to buy, at cut prices, the seats which are unbooked just before departure.

The first problem is to settle how large a discount from the 'going' fare for a particular service is necessary to compensate for the uncertainty; for the chances of getting a seat in these conditions will vary enormously from day to day and from service to service. However, with many business and holiday journeys, *any* degree of uncertainty is unacceptable. So the market which is available to be tapped by such devices is probably not considerable.

The second problem, and the one that matters most to the airline, is the possibility of diverting traffic, that would have paid the booked fare, to the stand-by fare, thus upsetting the whole economics of the operation. This is a real danger as it is most liable to happen to the commuter business traffic (which is the back-bone of many domestic services), because it is extremely knowledgeable about particular timings or days which tend to be lightly loaded.

Obviously, any scheme of this kind must be accompanied by cancellation fees for booked seats, at least equal to the difference between the stand-by fare and the booked fare, otherwise booked passengers can arrive at the airport, find the aeroplane is only half full, and cancel out their reservation before buying a stand-by ticket!

To digress a little at this point, the international airlines in their IATA agreements have been unable to maintain agreement on cancellation charges, or even on charges for people who book and simply fail to turn up ('no shows'). The Association discovered fairly early in its life that merely having agreements did not ensure their observance. The honest airline was in a particularly bad position. It charged the agreed rates and fares, weighed all baggage and insisted on excess charges being paid even for one kilo, kept to the stipulated meals standards, scrupulously excluded freight from the special commodity rates unless it fell precisely within the agreed descriptions, and so on. The unscrupulous airline, to attract traffic, simply broke the regulations. So the Association has set up enforcement procedures, and heavy fines are imposed on airlines found to have broken the agreements which they freely entered into at the Traffic Conferences.

It may be asked why any airline should behave in this way. The answer is simply that the airline which is doing badly in competitive conditions and has poor loads is liable to go to great lengths to secure traffic. The regular travellers soon discover which airlines do, and which airlines do not, worry over-much about excess baggage, and this alone can swing a useful proportion of the traffic. But the whole advantage in the end comes down to the simple situation that, where several suppliers are all charging the same price and maintaining the same service standards, the one who improves on these (from the customers' point of view) is bound to do well.

Apart from infringements with what might be called, at best, the tacit approval of Head Office, sheer administrative inefficiency in informing, instructing and controlling staff can produce the same effect. Moreover, all airlines are at the mercy of their staffs in this, as in other, respects. Area sales offices (particularly those geographically remote from, and therefore infrequently visited by, Head Office) may, of their own volition, infringe IATA regulations, within the bounds set by the accounting system, in pursuit of sales targets which seem unattainable by more orthodox methods. Against this background (apart from other quite real difficulties connected with problems of collecting penalties in the case of interline traffic, credit transactions etc.), the resistance to a cancellation and/or no show penalty in IATA is due to the fact that such a regulation would be very difficult to police, and quite easy to evade by some fairly simple book-cooking in the reservations office. The same arguments apply to a special fare for unbooked (stand-by) passengers.

A personal view on *late* cancellation and no-show charges is that it is a sad commentary on inter-airline co-operation that these cannot be introduced. The volume of no-shows on many international routes is frighteningly high, which must mean that on many occasions bookings are refused that could, in fact, have been accepted. Furthermore, cancellations which cost nothing lead to complete casualness in such matters on the part of passengers, so that a service departing with eighty passengers may have involved 200 bookings and 110 cancelling operations (apart from ten no-shows) with all the costs that this implies.

It is obvious that if an answer could be found to this problem, load factors would be improved and reservations costs reduced, so that the way would be open to fare reductions in the interest of the passengers. A personal, but perhaps optimistic, view is that effective no-show charges will eventually be agreed, because the present situation makes no sense; hopes of effective international cancellation charges are much more slender.

To return to the British domestic stand-by fare experiment—for it was clearly announced as such—the fare reduction given was one-third and appropriate booking and no-show fees were introduced at the same time. The stand-by fares were limited to routes with high average load factors (so giving a fairly high degree of uncertainty about getting away on a particular service) and with high frequency (so increasing the certainty of travelling some time on the chosen day). Obviously, so long as dilution remains *below* two-thirds, extra traffic more than compensates for that diverted from full fare to stand-by. BEA, which took the initiative in introducing these fares, did not have a monopoly on all the routes in question, but it did dominate them to a very substantial degree, which overcame any problems of the kind that worry IATA airlines in regard to the activities of competitors.

In their Annual Report for 1963–64 BEA stated 'these fares have helped to improve BEA's load factor without affecting the ability of the regular traveller to obtain a firm reservation at full fare'. However, research demonstrated that dilution was not inconsiderable and in late 1964 BEA applied to the Air Transport Licensing Board to reduce the discount. This was refused. A second application was successful, and the discount was reduced to 20 per cent from April 1, 1966.

An even more recent attempt to fill unbooked seats is the Youth Fare introduced in 1966 by certain (but not all) United States domestic carriers. The discount is 50 per cent, on a strictly stand-by basis, available to young people between the ages of 12 and 22 on production of an Identity Card which is supplied by one or other of the airlines in the scheme. As, at the time of writing, the Youth Fare had only just been introduced its effects cannot be judged.

CHAPTER VII

CO-OPERATIVE AGREEMENTS BETWEEN AIRLINES

———————

Chapters III and VI looked at those aspects of external control which limit the freedom of an airline to operate and price its services. The result is a situation which, in effect, imposes a very severe curb on the competitive processes to which the Western world is accustomed. The apparatus of Government bilateral air agreements and price fixing through the IATA machinery, is not infrequently criticised on the basis that the public would be better served if there were 'more competition'. IATA in particular, when wearing its fare and rate agreement clothes, is a constant target for such criticism.

The approach to the regulation of air transport typified by the Bermuda style agreement (including the price control clauses), or something less liberal, is the environment in which civil aviation operates today and is likely to continue to operate in the foreseeable future.

Since the object of this book is limited to an examination of the marketing management implications of the air transport scene, as it is and as it is developing, no attempt will be made to argue the pros and cons of regulation. Stephen Wheatcroft's *Air Transport Policy* already referred to, is a specific and recent critical examination of the whole field; his chapters III and IV deal in particular with the logical foundations on which the regulatory structure has been erected.

Within this framework, however, are also found agreements which are concluded between two or more international carriers, and which have the effect of limiting still further the impact of competition. These commercial agreements—often referred to as pooling agreements—though their genesis may differ in individual cases, usually represent a calculated marketing production policy on the part of those airlines party to them.[1] Commentators are usually highly suspicious of these agreements, and tend to regard them as com-

---

[1] They may serve the further purpose of interpreting the capacity clauses of the Air Agreement, since Government consultation to this end is usually dilatory.

pletely negating the limited amount of competition which the over-all international situation permits.

From the earlier chapters, and particularly Chapter VI, it is obvious that however skilfully an airline schedules its services and constructs its tariff, all the seats and all the hold space will not be full all the time. In fact, the amount that runs to waste is very great indeed.[1] The load factors of all ICAO members combined since 1954 demonstrate this clearly, and are set out in Table 8.

TABLE 8. *Combined load factors of all ICAO members. 1954–64*

	1954 %	1955 %	1956 %	1957 %	1958 %	1959 %	1960 %	1961 %	1962 %	1963 %	1964 %
Scheduled International Passenger load factor	57·7	60·4	61·7	61·3	56·7	59·6	58·8	53·0	52·1	51·8	54·8
Over-all load factor	60·1	60·6	61·4	60·5	57·5	59·7	57·9	52·5	52·1	51·8	53·5
Scheduled Domestic Passenger load factor	62·1	63·0	63·1	61·1	59·6	60·4	59·0	56·8	54·4	55·0	56·6
Over-all load factor	58·5	58·3	58·2	55·8	55·5	55·4	53·4	50·9	49·6	49·2	49·1

As an indication of the difference that a few points in load factor can make, with operating revenues in 1964 of $8,238 million and an over-all load factor (international and domestic combined) of 51·1 per cent, each point of load factor was worth to the ICAO members as a whole, some $160 million.

Figures issued by IATA relating to its member airlines show how this 'wastage' can vary between traffic areas and change drastically from year to year; examples are given in Table 9.

TABLE 9. *Passenger load factors of IATA member airlines for selected traffic areas in 1963 and 1964*

	1963 %	1964 %
North Atlantic	49·1	57·5
South Atlantic	54·6	57·0
Intra Europe	55·6	55·2

In international conditions (and it is in international air transport that commercial agreements of the type under review are found), Government Air Service Agreements are normally written in such a way as to prevent the airline of one country ruining the airline of the

---

[1] For a comprehensive review of this problem, see 'Wasted Seats in Air Transport', by A. H. Milward, being the Brancker Memorial Lecture to the Institute of Transport, delivered on February 14, 1966.

other country in the long run. However, differences of opinion and differences of practice may well lead to particular airlines over-scheduling in the opinion of other airlines. As the Air Service Agreements work on the basis of an *ex post facto* review in the case of complaint, this must mean the possibility of a whole season, at least, of low load factors before a Government can be persuaded even to *begin* to intervene.

Resolution of such problems can never be easy, quite apart from the fact that a Government may not be anxious to quarrel with another Government about air transport matters, for reasons quite unconnected with civil aviation. If the logic of tariff-making and costing outlined in Chapter VI is accepted, one airline may be content to cover less of its overhead on a particular route than the parallel operator, and this may emerge (as both will be charging the same tariff) in the amount of capacity it mounts. All this may occur quite irrespective of whether one airline is more efficient (has lower true unit costs) than the other.

But all airlines are not dominated by purely commercial—profit-making—motives. An airline might be supported by its Government for prestige reasons, with losses accepted and met by subsidies of one kind or another. In this situation, and even against the background of a Bermuda-type bilateral agreement, such an airline could operate at just sufficient excess capacity to produce uneconomic load factors for the parallel operator, but not with sufficient excess capacity to call into play action by the Government of the other airline.

Yet another possibility exists. An airline, motivated by the most rigorous commercial approach, may be prepared to operate a short international route into its main base at low load factors with the object of offering high frequency connections on to its long-haul service. By any normal standards this service may be operated at a loss, taken on the basis of route costings, but the losses on this short-haul service may be written off against the additional revenue obtained for the long-haul service. The other airline operating the short-haul service in parallel, as part of its main network, particularly if its end of the route is a better traffic generating area than the other, is faced with an excessive capacity situation and low load factors with no compensating long-haul traffic.

As a matter of interest, in principle these problems are very similar to those that arise in road haulage, where the empty space on offer by hauliers who have carried load *into* a town can seriously affect the market for haulage *from* that town. Within a national state such problems can be met (perhaps only partially, but few transport problems of this kind can be completely resolved) by action on the part of the appropriate regulatory body.

Shipping conferences, unlike IATA, actually include capacity control in varying degrees in their agreements.

A tendency to excess capacity, leading to depressed profit margins, is always inherent in transport, and airline pooling agreements are no more than one answer by the industry to this problem.

If the airline industry were highly profitable at existing load factors, the urge to find ways and means of raising them, or even of keeping them from falling, would perhaps be less strong. But, as a whole, the industry teeters on a knife-edge of commercial viability. The ICAO figures show that, from 1954 to 1964, the world's scheduled airlines made actual operating losses in 1957 and 1961, and the highest profit (in 1964) was 7·8 per cent of the operating expenses, and this was quite exceptional. But, of course, one of the reasons for the low profit is this very tendency to excess capacity.

Commercial agreements involving the pooling of revenue are most commonly found in Europe, but by no means exclusively so. The circumstances which produce each of the pools may be any one or a combination of the factors outlined above, and the terms will differ in each case. Being commercial agreements, the details are confidential and so are not published. One can, however, describe in general terms the broad lines which a normal agreement of this kind will follow.

The object being to ensure that the capacity is controlled, the purpose of the agreement must be to define the amount of capacity each partner operates for the period of the agreement, and this must be preceded by an agreed forecast of the total traffic that is likely to be available on the route in question.

Where the operations are controlled, governmentally, by a Bermuda-type Air Services Agreement, and both parties to the commercial agreement are strong, developed airlines, it is likely that the agreed capacity split will be 50 per cent each, or something very near this.

Having agreed the traffic forecast and the shares of capacity, the next, and most vital, figure to agree is the load factor at which the partners will aim, since this will determine the total capacity required.

At this point the suspicious critic probably sees the cloven hoof appearing, and expects the agreement to aim at high load factors offering fat profits to the operators. Firstly, these agreements have existed, in Europe particularly, for very many years, and no European carrier is exhibiting excessive profits. Most have been, and are, showing quite modest returns on their capital with occasional lapses into the red. Secondly, a very high *average* load factor (for it is the average load factor which forms the basis of the agreement) must mean days on which the loads offering are so high that traffic is turned away. Any airline must experience this situation on odd occasions, but if average loads are running well over 70 per cent, the number of services which potential travellers find fully booked will normally be quite considerable, and unless an airline frequency is high (say six or more daily) the result of such load factors will be unsatisfactory customer relations. It will also mean loss of traffic to alternative operators, probably indirect air operators who are not included in the agreement. For example, if BEA and Alitalia were to attempt to screw load factors on London–Rome up to such heights, traffic would flow indirectly over Amsterdam, Paris, Brussels and Zürich, as well as by the other direct carriers, of whom there are several in this particular case.

In any case, these are agreements; both parties have to accept the planning assumptions. In the light of circumstances such as have been reviewed earlier in this chapter, one of the airlines at least is certain, for its own reasons, to be unwilling to press load factors too high because of the lower frequency this must produce.

From the agreed planned load factors the operating pattern of services can now be constructed. At this point a pooling agreement does open the door to serving the total market better than competition, and improving public service in the process. A route which has a demand capable of supporting only one direct flight daily in each direction, in straight competitive conditions, is almost certain to have (at least) four flights a week by each of the two national carriers concerned. This means eight weekly instead of the 'economic' seven. Moreover, each will fly on the best traffic days (each day of the week is unlikely to be equally productive), so leaving at least some days uncovered, during which the traffic that does want to move will almost certainly go with indirect carriers, thus reducing the total market available to the two direct operators. With higher frequency too—say two or three daily—the same argument will apply to timings, with two aeroplanes leaving within minutes of each other, and then a gap of hours.

Pooling cannot completely rationalise two airlines' parallel operations. There are too many other factors inherent in the operating capabilities and economics of both to permit every pooled route to be a model of joint scheduling. But, once a pool exists, self-interest dictates that both carriers will *want* to serve the market in partnership, and the final schedules are much more likely to give good public service in an economic manner than would be the case if the pool did not exist. The reason for this is that, having agreed the schedules to be operated, the revenue (after certain deductions) is pooled and divided in accordance with an agreed formula, the simplest being a straightforward division according to the capacity each partner operates during the period of the agreement.

Does this imply that all competition has now disappeared? Can one airline sit back and take its share without trying too hard to market its wares? Worse still, can both airlines sit back? The answer is undoubtedly 'no' to these, and any other questions of a like nature. However long the term of such agreements in principle, they obviously have to be vitalised season by season with the setting of the schedules. On each such occasion the partners will know the financial effects of the pool over the previous season. If one consistently pays large sums over to the other, or others, and there are no compensating factors, such as an earlier agreement that the lower revenue airline(s) will take the worst days or times, later scheduling periods will not be agreed very readily. No airline goes into pool for the pleasure of paying over large sums from its own traffic revenue. If the agreement actually survives in such circumstances, the financial clauses are likely to be re-worded so that a ceiling is put on the amounts that can be transferred. The 'inefficient' airline now no longer gets its full share of the revenue in accordance with capacity operated, but something less.

The other case—both airlines comfortably relying on capacity control to look after all their problems—is also unrealistic. It assumes firstly a 'natural' market for air travel between the two points served by the pooling airlines, and the opening chapters of this book should have dispelled any idea that a growing air travel market exists irrespective of what the airlines do to serve and develop it. Secondly, the indirect carrier is almost always around, eager to capture traffic from the ill-served direct market, whilst many routes will also have other direct carriers.

In short, a pooling agreement only works satisfactorily if, over the long term, each partner contributes its proper share of capacity and carries its share of the business, which automatically hypothecates competitive aircraft, frequencies and timings. Short term inadequacies by a partner are acceptable to the other only when there is an obvious remedial plan in the long term.

Of course, none of this means that there cannot be such a thing as a bad pool, unnecessary, ineffective, not in the public interest; nor that pooling could be the saviour of every uneconomic route. The arguments presented here are set out with the object of showing that a well-conceived pool can strengthen the economics of the airlines concerned, which must be valuable in its own right having regard to the over-all industry profitability problem. Just as important, immediate advantages can accrue to the public from an improved spread of schedules, and later advantages due to improved route economics permitting lower fares.

Although pooling agreements are basically production management devices, they are built on commercial factors as part of the over-all marketing plan; but they do present the day-to-day marketing side with not inconsiderable problems. On the one hand they release energies and resources from the relatively sterile process of selling almost exclusively *against* the parallel operator, for the infinitely more rewarding process of developing the market as a whole. But on the other hand, because each partner must keep his own end up in the pool, the persuasive elements in the marketing team cannot ignore the need to sell their own airline within the total pool concept. At no time can their approach be based on the idea that it is of no importance which of the pooled airlines the traffic chooses. Apart from the possible implications on the agreement itself if too casual an approach is made to the way the traffic splits between the partners, any airline must constantly preserve its identity if future traffic on *all* routes is to be maintained and developed.

The essence of commercial agreements of the kind described is that the total revenue accruing on the route is divided between the partners in relation (normally) to the capacity offered, irrespective of the volume of traffic carried by each. But each partner completely carries its own costs. In certain conditions, usually arising from an overriding political consideration or a particular external competitive situation relating to the national airlines concerned, a revenue pooling agreement of this kind may develop into a much closer association. In these cases the route—or more often a complex of routes—is operated by the two airlines under an agreement which also brings costs into the equation. They retain their identities, fleets and staffs, etc., but draw agreed cost allocations from the revenue pool before it is divided in accordance with capacity.

The simple inter-company hire of aircraft is almost exclusively a production matter, but such arrangements take on a strong marketing aspect when, for example, one company operates a service six times a week, and hires three of them out to another operator with rights on the route. Such an arrangement is normally made to keep marketing identities alive and could well be associated with a revenue pool, though this is not essential to such an agreement.

In the case of all the kinds of agreement which form the subject of this chapter, the dynamic behind them is economic—a desire to improve the unit production cost situation. But all have considerable influences, as has been shown, on the marketing side. In many ways they complicate the marketing task and certainly make the final settlement of the schedules, on which marketing is based, more difficult because of the need to reach agreement. Even after that has been done, it is not easy concurrently to promote the whole route *and* retain airline identity.

On the other hand, there is much less likelihood of finding the parallel operator breaking IATA agreements if he is in pool, whilst the improved economics arising from higher load factors enable fares and rates to be lower in the long run than they would otherwise be, with a consequent stimulating effect on the whole marketing process.

Two other important types of co-operative agreement between airlines affect the marketing side. These are the multilateral agreements between IATA members for the interline acceptance of traffic documents, and the General Sales Agency agreements sometimes concluded bilaterally between airlines. Both of these fit better into the sections of the book which deal with the marketing processes as such, whereas the revenue pooling agreements are better considered at this point, leading into the following chapter.

CHAPTER VIII

PRODUCT PLANNING

Marketing, as a conditioning agent in management thinking, should produce a consumer oriented business; the definitions which opened Chapter III all point in this direction. And the management of any business, on being asked if this were so in its particular case, would almost certainly, and probably indignantly, reply affirmatively. An ordinary 'capitalist' business would claim that in no other way could it maintain sales, and so remain profitable; a publicly-owned concern, or even a privately-owned public utility, would metaphorically place its hand on its heart and claim that its sole *raison d'être* was to serve the public; it might even go on to claim that any lack of profits observable in its finances was due entirely to the necessity of providing services *needed* by the public, but incapable of being provided at a cost which the public, as users, were prepared to meet.

Civil aviation may exhibit, in particular places and circumstances, aspects which call for criteria—other than the strictly economic—being used in making judgments as to whether services should be operated or not. The most obvious cases of this kind are seen in what are called the social air services in Great Britain—those services which connect the sparsely populated highlands and islands of Scotland with main centres of population. Similar circumstances exist in the USA and in Australia, where communities also exist whose demand for air transport, in money terms, cannot support air services in an exclusively profit-seeking environment.

If a decision is made to provide air services in these cases, this is a political decision, whoever makes it. It is not really the function of an air transport manager to decide that the social needs of a community for air transport are worth so much money, which will need to be defined in maximum terms at least, and which will be found from the profits earned by other air services.

Basically, air transport managements should set out to provide efficient services where demand, as expressed by willingness to purchase, exists, and do their best to provide the kind of services that the market requires. Airlines which are financed by private

F

capital operate, of course, precisely in this way. They have no mandate from their stock-holders to diminish the profits that would otherwise be earned by maintaining services which lose money, however socially desirable.

At first sight, it may seem that airlines owned by Governments will necessarily operate to a different set of rules. They may do and, indeed, some of them appear to do so, but there is no reason why State-owned airlines should not operate with the same motivation as privately-owned airlines; indeed, if the scarce capital resources of the world are to be most efficiently used, it is important that the capital-intensive airline industry should closely concern itself with return on investment. It is particularly important for State-owned airlines to be managed in this way, since the need to keep stock-holders happy and the money market eager to invest (in the absence of both of which a money-market financed airline will fail), is absent.

If the political and management decisions are kept separate, a State-owned airline can be put on exactly the same footing as the others. All that is required is:

(a) The airline management must be told that it is to operate as a commercial concern.

(b) If the State requires services to be operated that a commercial undertaking would reject, these particular services should be the subject of a special payment of compensation for the losses involved. In this way the needs of the traffic or community in question are assessed politically, and met out of *general* taxation, and not by random and accidental cross-subsidisation from profitable services.

Of course, all this is not quite so simple in practice. Airline costing does not make the exact calculations of losses or profits, on particular routes or groups of routes, easy to define in exact terms. But any State that wants its airline to be managed with the maximum of efficiency and concern for the customer must be well advised to block up all the funk-holes that the management can run to in explanation of bad performance.

British practice, which demands a commercial approach from its State airlines, accepts cross-subsidisation but meets the requirement of separating political from management decisions. The Government, as the owner, sets a target rate of return on capital lower than that normally earned by industry, in recognition of social and other 'wider obligations' carried by the State airlines (see Chapter III). Whatever the demerits of this approach, at least it is administratively simple and still leaves the management with the incentive to run a commercial airline.

The great majority of airlines, however capitalised, are required by their owners to operate commercially. Even where State subsidies meet continuing losses, the tendency is for pressure to be on managements to reduce and eliminate such losses. And in the long run this can only mean providing a service which people will want sufficiently for the costs to be covered by the fares and rates they pay.

So all airlines are faced with exactly the same interrelated set of problems as any other producer of goods or services. They must endeavour to produce what is saleable and not merely try to sell what is easily produceable. On the other hand, the ordinary facts of production will set limits to possibilities. The transatlantic journey for £5 is eminently saleable, but not a practical target to set production. The end result, as with any business, will have to be a compromise between market requirement and the physical and economic limitations on production. But it is still important that the airline should start with the consumer, and not the other way round.

If all this sounds very obvious it is because concern for the consumer has become a management cliché which it is not respectable to deny; but it may sometimes get overlooked in practice. Such aberrations may be manifested, when the marketing side wants something difficult, by rationalisation of the production point of view as being what the customers really want. What airline marketing man, too, has not been told at some time or another, when complaining of a poor product, that it is a challenge to his selling ability—any fool can sell a good product!?

But the marketing man *is* a fool if he thinks the most able and helpful production team in the world can give him everything he wants, even within the price scales he knows he must accept. The over-all production schedule is so complex, and improvement in one direction so often leads inevitably to deterioration in another, that the feed between marketing and production, to secure the most effective compromise, is more important and must be more continuous than in most other businesses.

The airline has resources, mainly aircraft and people, which it can deploy in a variety of ways. However, the freedom of deployment at any moment of time has certain limitations. For example, it is unusual for an airline of any size to be able economically to operate all its services with one aircraft type. There is, therefore, a restriction on the interchangeability of aircraft and crews between routes. Nevertheless, considerable flexibility does exist even in the short term planning stage.

With the peak/trough variations that exist in demand, it is common practice in most parts of the world to plan the production on offer—that is the timetable—on a summer and winter basis separately. In European conditions, the airline summer is from

April 1st to October 31st (seven months) and the winter is from November 1st to March 31st (five months). Programme planning in detail is, therefore, done twice each year and each plan will include shadings within the seasonal programme to meet traffic variations. For instance, April, July and October will not require the same number of services to holiday points as the other summer months. All these services must be planned and offered *in detail* in advance. The importance of this has already been stressed.

Within the volume and type of aircraft carrying capacity offered on each route, other 'quality' decisions will have to be made also; essentially these are the decisions relating to timings.

An airline produces a very large range of quite different services. These differences are not merely demonstrated by the various sector journeys offered, such as London to Brussels, Brussels to London, Manchester to Glasgow, but also in the date or time of use. So far as meeting demand is concerned, these differences are often, but not always, as great as the differences between soap and cheese. A business man going to Athens cannot be expected to go to New York instead if all the seats to Athens have been sold. Nor will he go on Wednesday if his business appointment is on Tuesday. He *might* go on a less preferred timing that will still get him to the place he wants in time for his appointment, but he won't even do that if another airline can offer him the time that suits him best. The holiday-maker, on the other hand, may be persuaded to go to a holiday destination other than the one he prefers if there is no space (by any airline), and he may abandon his July holiday if it is made attractive to him to travel in May.

All this has to be forecast in its volume implications and the time-table that the airline puts out each season is its assessment and 'offer'. Apart from the importance of reasonably accurate forecast of demand, the reflection of this in the schedules must also be accurate; close liaison between marketing and production in the fixing of the timetable is, therefore, of paramount importance.

The process, in its logical steps, can best be demonstrated by looking at the way in which a new service would be considered. In fact, although short cuts would be sensible in setting the whole programme of services, including decisions as to what expansion or otherwise should be scheduled for routes previously operated, the same basic considerations apply to every decision that is taken to operate a scheduled service.

Firstly, all the considerations inherent in market research and its concomitants must lead to the conviction that there is a demand, and this will be calculated. This calculation will take into account the competition that exists (or will exist at the operative time), fares or rates structures (existing or desirable) and indeed the whole potential saleability, in realistic price terms, of the projected service so far as the airline is concerned.

The controls that exist externally must next be considered. Do the desirable fares or rates exist, or can they be negotiated through IATA or the appropriate Government machinery? Similarly, as regards the inclusion of that route in the appropriate Air Services Agreement, and/or in the airline's portfolio of Government licences (if such are needed), this either is no problem, a difficulty or an insuperable barrier. The terms of any commercial agreement with other airlines may also be relevant at this stage.

Given that no snags have arisen on these considerations, from the point of view of demand and 'permissibility', the airline has a potential service and it will be possible to calculate the revenue to be expected from its operation in the planning period under review.

Whatever the organisational arrangements which apply in a particular airline, the next stage is a production assessment—the physical possibility or otherwise of mounting the service. This primarily requires consideration of the fleet and crew position, having regard to other requirements of the airline's total operating programme; but it may also require consideration of other factors, such as airfield limitations, prohibitions on night jet operations at certain airports, etc.

Provided, then, that the operation is feasible, the next step will be to cost it and compare the cost with the expected revenue.

What follows is crucial, as it conditions to a considerable degree the *quality* of the final decision.

Some projects may die as soon as cost and revenue are compared, for the adverse balance may be so great that, even looking into the future and allowing for development, the marketing side is satisfied without further discussion that the operation is basically not viable and should be dropped. Others may look so good that they can be agreed for the programme without further discussion or adjustment. This is particularly likely to be true over a large part of a developing programme, where it is merely a question of adding frequencies from a growing fleet to meet traffic expansion.

But there will inevitably be a grey area in which decision-making will not be simple. A new service may show a potential initial loss, leading to a profit after a certain period of operation. The current over-all profitability of the airline will be a dominant consideration in deciding how many (if any) such developing services can be carried at any one time. Production may not be able to offer the exact service (in volume, timing, aircraft type) which the estimates require for their fulfilment, necessitating a feed-back for recalculation of revenue. It may be possible to meet a particular requirement but, due to limited resources, only at the expense of some other requirement. This may be a direct choice between two different operations as alternatives, or a choice between a good time for one and a 'bad' time, commercially, for the other. Production may be able to meet the requirement completely, but may suggest a way of meeting it less adequately which will substantially reduce the costs.

This is the point at which careful calculation of all the pros and cons of the alternatives available must be weighed and the best compromise achieved. This is the marketing/production dialogue. It is too easy to say that every decision should be made on a comparison of cost and revenue. This must be the basic criterion, but some decisions relate to more revenue here or less revenue there, and the same with cost. Overriding considerations peculiar to the airline's situation may also, at times, require some services to be maintained temporarily although the economics are unsatisfactory. Such decisions should normally be made only after clearance with top management, who should certainly keep them under review lest they outlive their rationale and slowly bleed the airline to death.

This process of programme planning in its logical steps can be presented diagrammatically, as in figure 2 opposite.

It is perhaps worth emphasising that the programme planning processes which have been described will assimilate all requirements, however they may arise. Reference was made earlier in the chapter to the possibility of services being operated under other than straightforward marketing pressures, such as social services not meeting their full costs from the revenues directly attributable to them. However these may be financed, whether by direct Government subsidy or in any other way, they form a fixed framework round which the commercial services must be fitted. But provided such services only form a relatively minor portion of the network, the incentive to the airline will exist to operate them as economically as possible to release resources for the profitable services.

Much the same applies to services with timings dominated by mail requirements. On the whole the world's post offices are not particularly chauvinistic in their choice of carrier, and will move the mails by services that best meet their collective arrangements and give speediest delivery to addressees at the other end. If there are two services between any pair of points, the one that meets this requirement best will get *all* the mail, not just most of it.

Programme planning will, then, have to take into account the potential revenue from the mail, and any loss of revenue due to the timing being inconvenient for commercial load, as well as loss of revenue and good-will due to other load (particularly cargo) being constantly displaced. From this, a decision must be taken as to whether to cater for the mail or not.

The processes of programme planning are continuous in the

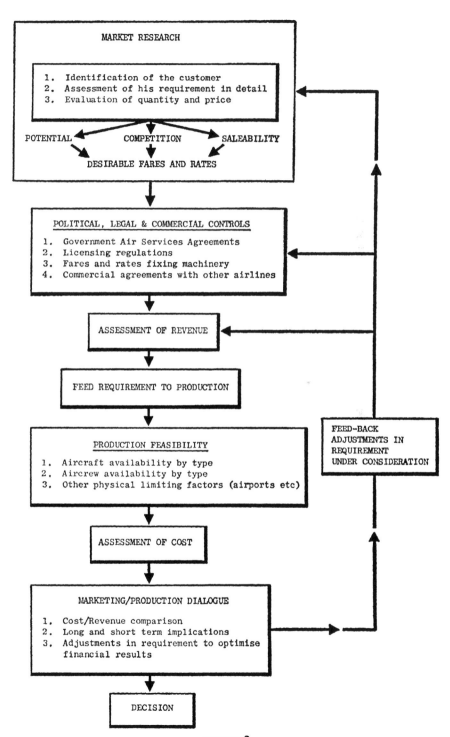

FIGURE 2

normal airline above medium size. With so many influences to evaluate—many of them constantly changing—and so many alternatives to weigh up, each season's programme will be up to a year in the making.

This short term seasonal deployment of resources in the optimum manner make up the tactical battle-orders which arise from strategic product planning decisions arrived at in the past.

An airline cannot normally make short term decisions to vary the numbers and/or basic characteristics of its fundamental production tools—aircraft and aircrew. Under-provision and over-provision, due to wrong forecasts as to total traffic available, can to a certain extent be overcome by charter. This possibility is very limited and uncertain and it also presents many problems compared with having just the right fleet, adequately crewed.

It is impossible to generalise on the time scale involved in forward provisioning for aircraft. Circumstances will vary enormously over time and for different airlines. Broadly, it is true that many airlines are carrying their traffic estimating forward for periods of five (in some cases even seven) years in order, *inter alia*, to plan the size and general type of fleet units they are likely to want. The time scale for air crew is shorter, but where no reservoir of pilots exists from the Services or elsewhere, and a large national airline has to ensure (with money) that young men are entering the profession, firm decisions may need to be made some two years ahead.

The planning of future fleets is not merely quantitative. At any moment of time an airline either has a highly competitive fleet or not. This will be the result, not only of its own previous decisions, but also of the historic decisions made by competitors. This kind of decision-making is true product planning.

Again, passenger aircraft will be ordered with interior layouts which seem, at the time of ordering, to meet the requirement as it will exist at the time of delivery. Apart from any changes that may be made in this specification, as date of delivery draws near and the requirement is seen more clearly, it is almost certain that during the life of a fleet, changing competitive conditions will call for changes in the layouts of existing fleets (seat configurations, pantry facilities, etc.).

A major decision in long term product planning affecting the interior layout of an airline's fleet relates to classes of service. In general, airlines offer not more than two classes of service which can be called tourist class and first class, though the nomenclature of the lower class varies around the world. Exceptionally, one finds three classes. The airline can ignore the first class and provide only tourist accommodation, but usually most try to offer both. Demand for first class being what it is, almost the only way to provide it without gross over-supply is to offer relatively small first class compartments in otherwise all-tourist aircraft. The ordinary mechanics of turning aircraft round speedily between flights, in order to maximise utilisation, make it extremely difficult to vary the size of the first class cabin from flight to flight. So the decision usually has to be taken to equip the cabins of all the aircraft of the type in a certain configuration (say eighty tourist and twelve first), and operate it this way, irrespective of fluctuating demand between the classes.

As a logical emanation of the fixed price situation in international air transport, as soon as there are two classes, each with its own fare level, what can be given in the lower class in particular must be defined. Without this the price differentiation would be nonsense. As the lower fare, to be economic, must be met by appropriate cost reductions per passenger carried, one of the essential features in the IATA regulations for tourist/economy class is a *maximum* seat pitch. This is the *distance* between the seats: seat width is controlled by specifying the number of seats *abreast* for each aircraft type. Obviously, the shorter the seat pitch the more seats can be fitted into a given fuselage, and the more potential passengers are available to share the costs of flying the aeroplane.

In this situation, variations in first and tourist class demand from service to service, when the configuration is fixed, cannot be met by allowing tourist bookings to spill over into unwanted first class seats. In such circumstances, the whole load factor problem is intensified and decisions, as to the number of each class of seat to be fitted in a given aircraft type, have to be taken with particular care. Moreover, as demand changes over time, it will be necessary to re-configure the aircraft to meet changed circumstances. BEA's Comet IV B's were introduced in 1960 with twenty-two first and sixty-four tourist seats. Two years later the configuration was eighteen first and sixty-nine tourist, a year later fourteen and seventy-four and, as this book goes to press, they have ten first class seats and seventy-nine tourist.

The short-haul airline has particularly acute problems in providing first class in this way. If a long-haul carrier has forecast demand reasonably accurately, since his fleet may well be allocated on a route basis (transatlantic, Europe–Far East, etc.) it is not likely that severe and *regular* fluctuations will occur from flight to flight. But a short-haul carrier, operating several different timings on the same route and different routes with the same aircraft, may well find that the morning flight A to B has heavy first class demand, the return flight during the day has almost no demand, and so on; also, that time on the ground between flights is inadequate for configuration changes. The problem is well exemplified by an actual integration in summer 1963 of a mixed class Comet IV B of the BEA fleet, as shown in Table 10 overleaf.

TABLE 10. *Summer, 1963, operating cycle of a BEA mixed class Comet IVB*

		DAY 1	Time on ground hrs. mins.				DAY 2	Time on ground hrs. mins.
London	dep.	0940			Nicosia	dep.	0010	
Rome	arr.	1150			Athens	arr.	0145	
			0	35				1 20
	dep.	1225				dep.	0305	
Athens	arr.	1410			London	arr.	0645	
			1	00				2 40
	dep.	1510				dep.	0925	
Nicosia	arr.	1640			Geneva	arr.	1050	
			0	45				0 55
	dep.	1725				dep.	1145	
Beirut	arr.	1805			London	arr.	1310	
			1	20				1 35
	dep.	1925				dep.	1445	
Nicosia	arr.	2015			Nice	arr.	1630	
			3	55				0 55
						dep.	1725	
					London	arr.	1915	

An interesting attempt to minimise this problem has been made by BEA, who have fitted their Trident fleet with first class seats which can be converted *in situ* to comply with IATA tourist class regulations.

A further complicating factor in fleet planning will be the provision to be made for cargo. To what extent should passenger aircraft be designed also to carry cargo; should specialised freighters be ordered; should an attempt be made to specify a passenger fleet which can be used with minimum conversion problems as pure freighters?

Many other aspects of airline planning cannot be called product planning, as they are derivatives of the major aircraft and route pattern decisions. Indeed this is true of aircrew planning.

But, over and above the forward thinking that goes into the shaping of the airline service within slowly changing traditional patterns, there must also be a readiness to break completely new ground.

The airline industry is not under the compulsion that exists in the consumer goods industries to introduce continuous innovations (or seeming innovations) in its product range. The opening up of new routes—which are the nearest thing to a brand-new product—is a form of expansion, but is not essential to the growth and economic well-being of an airline with a sound route network which it serves well. Only within limits are people who want to travel (for whatever reason) to point A, likely to be wooed away by 'whiter than white' type advertising to go to point B instead.

The development of airline service and the innovation that (*a*) keeps an airline in front of its competitors and (*b*) stimulates over-all demand, is on the whole more gradual and marginal. It is more truly product development than product innovation.

An outstanding example in the passenger field is the walk-on, no-reservation type of service. This undoubtedly has tremendous public appeal, as it relieves the passenger of many irritating processes in arranging and making his journey. From the airline's point of view, it interposes less people between the passenger and his objective— to get to the other end—so removing both costs and the chances of human failure. The only reason why this system has not spread rapidly is that few routes offer the potential depth of traffic to make it feasible and, even on heavily travelled routes, the economics are still somewhat suspect due to the depressed average load factor, which is an inevitable consequence of true guaranteed walk-on service.

In the freight field an example of product development is the introduction of specialised methods to handle particular items of cargo which otherwise would not move at all, or as readily—for example, garments on hangers.

To summarise, in setting the schedules, buying equipment, deciding on aircraft interior layouts, fittings and furnishings, catering day to day and service to service within the standards set by IATA regulations or company policy, and in many other short term or long term plans, decisions are being taken which affect the marketability of the airline's seats and hold space. If, in any particular airline, some or any of these decisions are made without reference to the marketing side as such, then it is either a case of the 'sell what you can make' philosophy or—more frequently—somebody who has no marketing responsibility making, unaided, decisions in which some evaluation of marketing problems and possibilities have played their part. And however capable he may be of doing this, it is wasteful and confusing to have two or more groupings of similar expertise working independently of each other. This is not to say that the marketing side necessarily make any of these decisions. But unless their' experience and advice is tied into product planning and development on all fronts, the airline is giving them a wonderful 'out' if sales are disappointing. Salesmen of reputable, repeat-purchase, goods and services *must* believe in their products, and the only way to ensure this is to provide, in the management echelons of the marketing side, formalised and coherent avenues of impact on the planning sections of the production side. Unless these are provided, comprehensively and consistently, the airline which claims to be consumer oriented simply is not.

CHAPTER IX

ATTRACTING THE CUSTOMER

The most obvious, costly and controversial method of attracting the customer is by advertising.

Discussion about advertising frequently attempts to differentiate between that which is informative and that which is persuasive. The economist tends to make a finer distinction, regarding informative advertising as necessary and useful, therefore an acceptable item of cost, and what he calls combative advertising as wasteful, raising costs above the necessary minimum. Many advertising men would scorn these differences and say that *all* advertising is intended to be persuasive, even the most coldly informative; if it is not, somebody is wasting the advertising appropriation.

Having said this, and nailing this book's colours firmly to the 'all advertising should be persuasive' mast, it is useful to have the three aspects—information, persuasion and combativeness—at least loosely separated in the mind when considering the whole problem of attracting the customer to the point of sale; particularly when deciding on the most appropriate message in any particular set of circumstances.

An airline cannot exist, or go on existing, unless people know that it exists. They must know where it flies and what prices it charges. Publicising these facts may be persuasive. On the other hand they may, simply as cold, unvarnished facts, be the opposite. 'Fly (would I like it?) to Ruritania (never heard of it) at a cost of £50 (can't afford it).' If the airline wants to sell any air tickets to Ruritania it will have to do better than this—it will have to persuade people. This may consist of using other facts. 'Few people are sick'; 'Few people are killed'. All very true but hardly persuasive. The real job to be done is to give people the urge to travel. Unfacts should never be used. But if the picture drawn is of a happy person not being sick, not being killed and enjoying the sun, is this untrue because a very few people *are* sick (often from excitement or apprehension), the fatality rate is 0·76 per 100 million passenger miles, and it does sometimes rain in Ruritania?

Whatever the message that is to be conveyed to potential customers, the means available can be broadly divided into three categories:

(*a*) Advertising, which can be defined to include all those aspects which involve buying into an existing means of communication with some section of the public. It covers, therefore, advertisements in newspapers and periodicals, hoardings and posters (the 'existing means' here is the site), television and radio commercials and the like.

(*b*) Sales promotion. This embraces a variety of methods which are distinguished from advertising only because the material is produced by the seller, and distributed to the selected section of the public by such channels as are available, including the mails. Examples are direct mail (letters personally addressed to prospects), timetables and fare and rate tables, and information booklets.

(*c*) Canvassing. This generalised, somewhat old-fashioned but useful omnibus word, is intended to include all personal calling by representatives of the seller on prospective buyers or agents. It would also include talks and lectures to a group of people.

The first problem facing the airline is not so much what to say, or even how to say it, but what total amount should be spent. At the beginning of the appropriate period (probably in the annual budget covering the forthcoming financial year), a decision has to be made as to the total appropriation for all these items. The first two will be expressed simply as amounts of money, possibly wrapped up in one over-all sum, whilst the third, although it too, of course, will be expressed in money must also be expressed in terms of staff numbers and organisation.

There is no rule of thumb on this, although formulae are often quoted such as: 'the advertising vote should not exceed x per cent of the total expenditure'. The conditions, the relative position of the airline and the media available in each of the markets served, will vary so enormously that formulae can be misleading. Even viewed in total, taking all the pluses and minuses inherent in the variety of markets covered by a large airline, there cannot be a percentage that is right for all cases.

The degree to which managements differ in their assessments of the amount to be allocated to this kind of activity can only be demonstrated indirectly. Airlines in the USA have to make detailed financial and statistical returns to the Civil Aeronautics Board, and a great deal of this is published. Table 11 overleaf shows the different situations even of airlines in the same basic market.

Whatever decision the airline management finally makes as to the

TABLE 11. *Major United States Airlines*

Advertising expenditure as percentage of Operating revenue
and Sales and Promotion Costs
YEAR 1963

| Airline | Advertising expenditure | | | Operating revenue | Sales and promotion costs | Sales and promotion costs as |
	$ '000s	% of operating revenue	% of sales and promotion costs	$ '000s	$ '000s	% of operating revenue
United	10,228	1·6	16·7	622,864	61,104	9·8
Pan American*	16,588	3·0	20·3	558,574	81,771	14·6
American	8,368	1·7	16·4	488,056	51,117	10·5
T.W.A.*	15,831	3·3	24·9	476,513	63,524	13·3
Eastern	8,501	2·4	20·6	354,989	41,293	11·6
Delta	5,892	2·8	26·5	209,818	22,213	10·6
Northwest*	3,600	2·1	21·2	168,824	16,985	10·1
National	3,833	3·5	28·0	110,441	13,712	12·4
Western	2,518	2·5	22·7	99,427	11,096	11·2
Braniff	2,385	2·4	21·8	98,476	10,924	11·1
Continental	2,471	3·2	35·5	78,267	6,961	8·9

* International or part-international carriers. Remainder basically Domestic Operators.

NOTES: *Operating Revenue*. Revenues from the performance of air transportation and related incidental services. Includes (1) transport revenues from the carriage of all classes of traffic in scheduled and nonscheduled services including the performance of aircraft charters and (2) non-transport revenues consisting of Federal subsidy (where applicable) and the net amount of revenues less related expenses from services incidental to air transportation. Includes *all* revenue.

Sales and Promotion Costs. Costs incurred in promoting the use of air transportation generally and creating a public preference for the services of particular air carriers. Includes the functions of selling, advertising and publicity, space reservations, and developing tariffs and flight schedules for publication.

Source. Advertising Expenditure—*American Aviation*, May 1964.

Operating Revenue   } Air Carrier Financial Statistics, Civil Aeronautics
Sales and Promotion Costs } Board, Washington, D.C.

total amount it is prepared to allocate to attract the customer, the marketing director is left with the task, not only of distributing this total amount between advertising, sales promotion and canvassing, but also of breaking each of them down still further into markets. An international airline serving a dozen different countries has to mount its promotional effort in each of these countries. All airlines, domestic or international, have to mount a promotional effort from each point served. It is at this point that the real problem begins, because it is extremely difficult, except in the very broadest sense, to measure specifically the revenue results of money spent on the various aspects of customer persuasion in a particular market.

One thing is clear, and that is the difference between advertising on the one hand and sales promotion and canvassing on the other.

In any market, so far as advertising is concerned, the traffic potential must be substantial enough for the particular airline to calculate that it is worth spending enough to reach the threshold of effectiveness. This is not just a question of coping with the competitive advertising of other airlines or other forms of transport, but spending enough to achieve any kind of impact against the background of *all* the other advertising to which the potential customer is exposed. One airline advertising manager has described this as penetrating the decibel curtain.

The minimum level of advertising expenditure to achieve impact in any given set of circumstances is largely a matter of expert judgment; it is certain that any advertising *below* this minimum will be ineffective. If, therefore, the potential for an airline in a particular market is small, it may well be that the threshold advertising effort is out of all proportion to the income obtainable. In such circumstances, the money available for promotional effort is much better spent on sales promotion and/or canvassing, where results can be achieved directly proportional to quite a small outlay.

Once the decision to advertise has been taken, and the over-all allocation agreed in money terms, the media to be used have to be selected.

Whether one is buying space in newspapers or periodicals, sites for hoardings or posters, radio or television time, the principle is the same—one pays for coverage. The greater the readership of the journal, the more people that walk past the site, the larger the number of listeners or viewers, the greater the cost for the same basic advertisement, measured in space or time terms.

But mere coverage, in numbers of people exposed to the message, is not the only factor the advertising manager has to consider in spreading his budget around. He also has to take into account the type of readership, etc. that the medium reaches. Taking two extremes as an example, a financial periodical and a magazine with direct appeal to children could have the same circulation, the latter offering advertising rates that work out much cheaper per potential reader (which is higher than the circulation because of multiple readership). But the potential travellers in the children group would be so few, and those in the financial group so large, that the magazine circulating among the former would probably not even be considered, and certainly not as an alternative to the financial periodical.

Airline tickets are relatively expensive things, and when appealing to the leisure market—as distinct from the business travel market— the tendency must be to use media that reach the wealthier strata in the society that forms the particular market. However, holiday travel by air does not correlate neatly with rising income. Apart from the market research evidence that exists to demonstrate that leisure travel is spreading into quite low income groups, and certainly includes today a substantial proportion of manual workers, it is also known that factors connected with the stages in the life-cycle of the average person exert pressures which distort any correlation of leisure travel and income.

All societies will have their own peculiarities in this respect, but the general pattern can be illustrated from the British scene.

Firstly, manual workers' wages and paid holidays are such that if the urge is there, leisure travel, including foreign travel and the choice of air transport, is possible at a very early age (late 'teens). The clerical group in the community reach the same situation a little later, whilst the professional group are not earning well until their late twenties. However, student grants are generous enough nowadays for many who are still at University to be able to afford travel in the vacations, though this market is very price-conscious and less comfort-conscious, making it difficult to attract to the scheduled airlines.

Marriage often makes little difference to this pattern, with the habit increasing, in all except the highest income ranges, of wives continuing to work. But the arrival of children stops travel.

From this point the ability to afford leisure travel, once the sheer immobility imposed by very young children has passed, typically reappears earliest among the manual workers. Firstly, they are more likely to benefit from cheap accommodation costs in the shape of, for example, housing owned by local authorities. Secondly, the wives are more likely to recommence working whilst the children are still at school. Thirdly, the children will all use free State education. The further up the income scale one moves, the more likely it is that the typical family will be buying a house, the wife will have ceased working, and in Britain the upper-middle and upper class habit of squeezing the family budget so that the children (the boys in particular) can go to a 'good school', will supervene. Of course, once the children are 'settled' (and, often concurrently, the house mortgage paid off), the upper income families are the best market of all for leisure travel—it is the typical goal of such families for the day when family financial responsibilities are behind them.

Mutatis mutandis, this kind of pattern is typical of a developed community and advertising, with its broad impact, has to be geared to the situation existing in the market which is being worked.

In many ways, the more precise instruments of sales promotion and canvassing, once the market has been analysed, can be organised in such a way as to minimise the waste inherent in advertising, which must fall on many deaf ears or blind eyes, whatever the care taken in media selection and however much expertise is put into devising the advertisement.

Although the term 'sales promotion' is often used to cover a variety of activities which are often little more than specialised advertising, it is convenient for analytical purposes to think of it as covering any non-personal and specific approach aimed at a group of prospects, *all* of whom can reasonably be expected to be susceptible to the message. The best example of what is meant by this is a special event mailing. The sales promotion section, discovering that there is, say, an international congress or trade fair covering a particular profession or industry at some point served by the airline, sets out to circularise the best list of known participants or potential participants it can obtain.

In more general terms, an airline will build up a mailing list of important customers, or of firms and organisations known to initiate or sponsor a good deal of travel or freight movement. This list of addressees will receive timetables as they change seasonally, as well as regular information about other developments in the airline (new routes opened, fare and rate changes, introduction of new aircraft types).

Personal canvassing, using an outside sales force, has an important part to play, but is quite different from outside selling as practised by the consumer goods industries. In the latter case, the men are calling on wholesalers, retailers and users, and actually selling to them—taking concrete orders. The scope for this is almost non-existent in the airline industry. The outside sales force is, therefore, engaged primarily in promoting and retaining business.

A large part of the force will be engaged in regular calls on the travel and cargo agencies, ensuring that they are adequately offering the services of the particular airline. Such calls, incidentally, clear up queries and complaints. Other men will be calling on firms which are large users of the airline's services, mainly to make certain that all the necessary information—persuasive information!—is available to the right people to ensure that business continues to flow in increasing quantity to the airline, but also to deal with enquiry, comment and criticism. The function is really not dissimilar in many ways to the regular contact any sensible firm maintains with a large user of its technical products. It is very much part of the basic marketing concept, keeping in close touch with the consumer in order that his requirements may be met. A third function of the outside force is in seeking new business. This is basically 'cold calling', perhaps initiated by a lead (for example, a newspaper story of a contract), designed to find and encourage new travel or freight movement by the airline. Speciality salesmen, moving in such fields as sport or entertainment, are examples of this kind of canvassing; such men most nearly approach the traditional idea of an outside

G

salesman, as they do literally conclude many of their calls by positively effecting an identifiable sale.

Returning to the general aspect of budgeting for all this activity, the problem of measuring the results of a particular advertisement, direct mail shot or personal call, is as acute in the airline industry as in any other and greater than in most. It is difficult to key advertisements as the message is not expected to bring orders in then and there for the specific item advertised. Even direct mail letters, hung on to a special event, may bring in bookings through any one of a hundred or more travel agents, none of them identifiable from the other people who were going to travel to that destination for quite different reasons. And the outside representatives have no order book from which their effectiveness can be judged.

Although at times it may be possible to make reasonably accurate judgments—for instance a coupon inserted in an advertisement for a holiday booklet—in the main those responsible for directing the various activities described in this chapter must use broad indications of their success or otherwise. Provided the necessary organisation is set up, every ticket and air waybill can be identified as to place of issue. Area, regional and individual office sales returns can, therefore, be analysed in any detail required, but the cost of this detail will be heavy. It will be a matter of judgment as to how much it is worth spending on this kind of control, and this again will depend on the volume of promotional expenditure that is to be controlled. But, if a reasonably detailed analysis is maintained, over time the effectiveness of each part of the promotional effort can be judged, provided that concurrently other factors, such as variations in the product and the competitive environment, are used as correctives.

Although most airlines, in their major markets, had always spent some (but not much) money on generalised cargo advertising, it was not usually regarded as very effective. In fact it sometimes took on the character of something to keep the Cargo Sales Manager happy, so long as he was satisfied with a few insertions in specialist periodicals! Cargo promotion was much more dependent on the cargo sales representative digging into the problems of capturing existing surface flows, and on sales promotion retaining the contact with the shipper who had been won.

Most major airlines who are seriously in the cargo business have realised that the development of air cargo is a much more complex matter than the development of passenger traffic (leisure or business), simply because the inducement factors range over such a variety of considerations. In effect, much cargo will only move by air if the total distribution costs become attractive, and the actual transport rate is but a part of this total.

An excellent example, taken, as it were, from real life, is shown in Table 12. It is taken from *Air Freight—Key to Greater Profit* by A. D. Groenewege and R. Heitmeyer.

TABLE 12. *Comparative costs of shipping a consignment by air and surface transport*

For a 2,400-lb. shipment of photographic equipment from Stuttgart to New York, the use of air cargo provides a saving in direct costs of $263.83 compared with surface transport (and the delivery time is 18 days faster). The complete break-down of costs and related items is as follows:

Direct costs	Air	Surface
Net weight	2,400 lb.	2,400 lb.
Gross weight	2,850 lb.	3,240 lb.
Cubic volume	189 cu. ft.	234 cu. ft.
Declared value for insurance	$21,600.00	$21,600.00
Door-to-door shipping time (average)	2 days	20 days
Packing or crating, including labour	$36.00	$140.40
Pick-up and delivery charges	$46.90	$52.30
Transfer charges	Nil	$13.50
Freight charges	$853.38	$730.20
Insurance	$27.00	$216.00
Documentation charges	$0.98	$11.25
Transit warehousing and wharfage	Nil	$12.60
Interest on capital	$5.76	$57.60
TOTAL	$970.02	$1,233.85

This has led to the setting up, within cargo departments, of 'advice bureaux', coupled with advertisements of the closely reasoned informative type ('seventeen ways X Y Z Airlines can increase your overseas profits') in appropriate media read by business men. The advertisements invite enquiries which are then followed up by the specialist outside men. This kind of advertising is measurable as to its effectiveness.

Although the main 'service' given is to analyse such cost aspects as packing, insurance, warehousing, inventory (the capital costs of stock holding), pilferage, breakage, etc., plus the advantages of speed, some go further by offering market analyses to potential shippers and even 'Your first new overseas sales approach—free'.

In the field of advertising, in particular, the market research manager can be of particular help to the advertising manager. Apart from his library of knowledge in regard to the disposition and origin of traffic, economic evaluations of particular markets and so forth, whenever he conducts in-flight surveys or commissions interview-research, it costs very little to add questions of value to the advertising manager—for example 'What papers/periodicals do you read?'

Looking at the over-all picture of what is involved in attracting the customer, an airline finds itself very much concerned with image-building, as well as conveying specific informative or persuasive messages. Prestige advertising, as such, is practised by all major airlines and is probably the cause of more arguments (particularly in Board rooms), than any other type of advertising.

Air transport is new enough, and its occasional disasters horrific (and front-paged) enough, to breed a degree of apprehension about flying in the minds of some people, which is greater than they would feel if contemplating a surface journey. However illogical, the slaughter on the roads leaves people certain that it won't happen to them; highly publicised air disasters in remote parts of the world make them believe that it just *might* happen to them. All this is linked with the relative newness of air travel and the consequent feeling (diminishing as old people retire to their rocking-chairs and young people grow up with air travel), that it isn't quite natural.

To any airline, this apprehension is a deterrent. To the major airline, operating to standards well above the minimum levels laid down by national legislatures, there is genuine sales promotional value in projecting an image of reliability, safety and stability superior to that of the marginal operators. The aim is to create an acceptable, or preferably an attractive, corporate personality.

Safety records, as such, are rarely advertised. Some would have it that this is a matter of superstition; the day one boasts of performance in this respect some unfortunate incident occurs. Perhaps this is not without some element of truth. The pagan belief that the fickle gods should not be flaunted lurks in the most sophisticated twentieth-century mind. However, whether it be rationalisation of the irrational or not, there is a more logical reason for not harping on about safety. Such advertising emphasis might create in the mind of the reader the very unease the advertisement is designed to remove, on the basis that if you underline safety, it must be because the whole thing is inherently unsafe. Besides, how many potential passengers, ignorant of the laws of chance, believe that it might be that airline's turn next?

However much one speculates about the content of the public mind on this question, the fact very much remains that small human errors or deviations from strict standards of maintenance and operation can have disastrous consequences. The modern aeroplane in heavy traffic conditions is very unforgiving, and only provides split-second time to recover from mistakes.

The object of prestige advertising is to build up confidence in all that lies behind what the public actually sees when it flies. At its most effective, it would induce the intending passenger to ask for the airline which has built up the best image in his mind for every journey he wants to undertake, instead of first finding out if it even goes there. Examples of this kind of advertising copy are:

'Each jet engine is stripped down to 2,000 parts during overhaul', accompanied by a laboratory-type illustration showing ball-bearings being clinically inspected in a dust-free room.

'Why we tell an XYZ crew when to work and when to rest', with detail on how crews are protected from fatigue.

'Practically every XYZ engineer is a science and engineering graduate.

'Your XYZ Commander is also a 14,000-hour pilot, a graduate engineer, and a licensed navigator.'

This kind of specific message is reinforced by a complete projection of the airline as sound, safe and reliable in its appearance and manner. The approximation of uniforms to those worn by navies and merchant services has some historical associations with the traditional qualities of sea-faring men. Industrial design is called in to round off the picture. Staff attitude training completes it. If it is all well done, it cannot be over-done.

In Chapter III the undifferentiated nature of the airlines' products was mentioned, and criticism is sometimes levelled at the advertising because it tries so hard to differentiate. Prestige advertising of the type just described is, of course, an attempt at differentiation. And there is no doubt that this is meaningful and can be effective.

Perhaps less easy to defend is the advertising which stresses the kind of service offered, simply because it tries to point a difference which is scarcely noticeable and because it is probably relatively ineffective, as any airline can—and does—make the same claims. It becomes a case of a battle of superlatives.

Nevertheless, service aboard (and on the ground—in many ways as important but much less stressed in airline advertising or developed in airline practice), is a favourite advertising theme. Some airlines appear to concentrate on it exclusively. But because the copy has to be imprecise, as it tries to create an atmosphere of good service which no catalogue of advantages can do, it is in very real danger of creating an impression which is not borne out by the facts.

Tourist/economy class service—and this is how the great bulk of the traffic moves—*has* to be relatively austere and impersonal, however excellent it may be of its kind. As a consequence, lyrical advertising can lead to expectations which, because of the level at which it is pitched, are disappointed. And this inhibits repeat sales. *None* of the following examples referred specifically to first class, so must be taken as referring to tourist/economy as well:

'XYZ offer you hospitality unique in air travel!'

'Relax and enjoy VIP treatment! International cuisine delightfully served!'

'The lavish service, luxurious surroundings and superb cuisine. . .!'

'Passengers . . . enjoy hospitality at its best, are pampered with top quality food, superb service!'

The introduction of a new aircraft type always calls for a particularly heavy advertising appropriation. This again is a form of differentiation, but a very important one which is essential. Many passengers *are* attracted by the newest equipment, simply because it is the newest. The airline's image as modern and an innovator is aided. And passengers who avoid flying by the airline simply because they prefer the equipment used by competitors must be tempted back.

A form of differentiation advertising commonly met, which has prestige aspects (because it implies size and, therefore, stability and operational spending power), but which is broadly informative, is the network coverage type:

'All round the world, at 71 cities, the big X Y Z jets come and go.'
'The giant X Y Z world network now serves 48 cities in Europe alone.'
'. . . calls at 82 cities in 47 countries.'
'. . . this summer seves all the top Ruritanian holiday resorts.'

and the more specific

'over 30 flights a week to Ruritanograd.'
'one of the largest European networks of any airline (350 flights a week, 47 cities served).'

All of these are designed to make people think of the airline wherever and whenever they want to go.

People who are troubled about truth in advertising probably accept that superlatives are used so commonly nowadays in all forms of advertising that they no longer mislead, and factual copy stressing size and coverage cannot be faulted in this respect at all. But the slanted fact *can* mislead, and is generally regarded as undesirable. The one way in which many airlines offend against this particular tenet is in advertising new low fares as though they alone offer them (without actually saying so) when, of course, every other airline is offering the same fare—'save money with X Y Z's new economy excursion fare of only . . .'

But the increasing trend in leisure travel advertising, because the journey itself is only the means to that end, is to concentrate on the delights of the destination, with the airline featured and associated but often hardly stressed. This is often combined with a coverage emphasis—'See the New York World's Fair and visit up to 20 USA cities at no extra fare on a X Y Z ticket to the West Coast, USA'.

It can be argued that a good deal of this promotional effort is wasteful, even that which successfully attracts traffic to one airline instead of another; the reasoning being that the real task is to extend the travel market and direct the consumer discretionary expenditure towards travel and away from other things. The short answer to this is that a good deal is wasteful in any sense of the word, as is a good deal of all advertising. The oldest story in advertising is that half the allocation is wasted, but nobody can identify which half. As to the advertising emphasis, the great change in the last few years is towards over-all travel promotion, and away from a total concentration on attracting the already committed traveller.

But there are real differences between airlines, and between air travel and other forms of transport, so that a certain amount of money spent on 'selling the difference' (provided that it is not illusory) must make sense. The passenger advantages in flying compared with surface travel are, in fact, being less emphasised than formerly, presumably because airlines assume they have the advantage of speed and some disadvantages of price, and not much more need be done about this because it is too well known, except to high-light fares reductions when they arise.

A glance at surface transport travel advertising indicates, for the mid-sixties, a refusal to accept decline and a determined effort to 'sell the difference' of surface transport by concentrating on advantages in slower and roomier forms of transport. For example, a shipping service between Britain and Europe—'the night boat . . . brings you all the comforts of a good hotel—and saves you money. There are fully stocked bars where you can enjoy a duty-free nightcap, comfortable lounges, excellent restaurants, plenty of room to take a stroll and breathe the fresh sea air before you turn in for a full night's rest. You wake relaxed and refreshed.' The transatlantic message is on the same lines of 'wrapped in comfort, consideration and serenity', with a by-line about secretarial services and radio telephones for the business men. The two aspects are neatly brought together in 'the ship does not *take* time, it gives it for your health and profit'. Domestic railway travel advertising tends to concentrate little on its advantages over other forms of public transport, preferring to try to win traffic back from the private car, which all over the world has been the principal cause of its loss of passenger traffic.

So, by and large, the airline's promotional effort cannot be based on an easy assumption that air travel is the growth market while surface travel is in decline. The battle has to be fought on quite a number of fronts at the same time—developing the urge to travel, ensuring movement is by air, and then steering it to the particular airline; and, of course, keeping what has already been won. This is not easy, and efforts to do too much can result in ineffective promotion merely because the attempt to do several things at once is badly co-ordinated. This complexity makes the problem of reaching a threshold even more difficult, because it may well be that the only really effective way of achieving the necessary variety of impacts on the market is to mount several series of advertisements in different media, or at different times, or to adopt other schemes (using sales promotion techniques or the outside sales force), the emphasis being changed for each campaign.

One thing is certain, the bumper advertisement, direct mail letter, or sales call, which endeavours to cover everything from aircraft type to car-hire service at the other end, via food, service, pretty stewardesses, fares, network, frequency and everything else, is bound to fail. The decibel curtain cannot be pierced by tedious blunt instruments, only by short sharp ones.

CHAPTER X

THE POINT OF SALE

Whatever the product, somewhere in the marketing chain there has to be the point at which the customer takes possession and pays over his cash. In some cases it may be a little more involved as a total process than in others, but some system of sales outlet has to exist.

Methods used will not only differ between products, but within the same broad product range manufacturers may not all use the same outlet method, or may use more than one. Generally, the systems in use fall within the following six categories:

(a) Sale to wholesaler who, in turn, supplies the retailer (the actual outlet to the public) e.g. clothing and watches.

(b) Sale direct to the retailer who resells to the public, e.g. grocery trade, confectionery.

(c) Sale through a tied, or owned, network of retail outlets, e.g. petrol, shoes, cars, beer.

(d) Direct sale from the factory to the public by:

(i) Door to door salesmen, e.g. brushes.
(ii) Advertisement (mail order) e.g. some consumer durables.
(iii) Individual order achieved by direct contact methods, e.g. industrial goods.

(e) Use of an agent, who holds no stock but sells on a simple commission basis, calling forward products as he sells them, e.g. houses.

(f) Direct sale to a manufacturer, who includes the component in his final product, e.g. tyres sold to car manufacturers.

The airline industry, in general, uses a complex of outlets which cover many, though not all, of the types enumerated above.

Before the aeroplane had even been invented there existed in all the developed countries a network of outlets for travel and transport, namely the passenger and cargo sales agents. Acting purely as agents, as in category (e) above, they sold all forms of travel, or all means of transport for which they could obtain the sanction of the principals concerned. Although to that extent they were (and are) retailers of passenger and cargo transport, their technical position in the marketing chain is quite different from that of a shop selling consumer goods, for in the latter case the retailer shares some of the risk with the producer, having paid for the stock on his shelves.

The earliest airline companies 'took over' this network (in the same way that a new entrant into the chocolate bar trade concentrates on existing confectioners), and set out to make agreements with all or most of them to sell seats on a commission basis. Because they had a new product which needed pushing, the tendency was to offer a higher rate of commission than that offered by surface carriers, as an inducement to the agents to exert themselves to sell air transport.

Even from the earliest days, since ground staff had to be situated at airports to receive and check in the passengers and cargo, it was possible to deal direct with the airlines. Booking systems had to exist, these grew in size and complexity and moved away from airports. As the volume of business grew in the towns and cities served by an airline, it was a natural development to open a sales office of the particular airline in these on-line places.

Off-line—that is in population centres not directly served—it is quite uncommon to find airline offices. The cost of a well-sited and staffed office is considerable and, even with a major airline, the volume of business coming to it from any point not directly on its route network is seldom sufficient to justify the cost. An airline office will always, of course, sell the particular airline much more vigorously and knowledgeably than an agent, with his dispersed loyalties and his need to know all about many airlines and other forms of transport. Additionally, a centrally situated town office gives the airline a shop window—in the literal sense—for self-advertisement and constant projection of itself. But unless the potential in the town is high, the cost per sale will be heavy and the airline will, perforce, have to satisfy itself by securing its local sales through the agents, and abandoning any idea of opening its own office.

The reservations office may or may not be in the same building as the town sales office. In fact, there is a good deal of sense in *not* having it there if the sales office is well sited, in the appropriate busy centre, for rents there are bound to be high. The reservations office merely needs good telephone, telex, etc., communication, and can be in an area of low site values. Since airline sales offices have to go to the reservations offices for seats etc., it is convenient for the public who telephone or write to do the same and not 'post office' such requests through the airline sales office which handles the personal caller. This has something of the character of the 'direct from factory to public' type of selling.

Many travel agents also function as tour operators, marketing a complete holiday at a set price, including (as a minimum) travel and accommodation, which is sold through their own offices and sub-agents. This is sometimes referred to as wholesaling, but is in reality closer to component selling and will be discussed in more detail later in this chapter. True wholesaling and true retailing are not found in the airline industry, although cargo consolidation—also expanded towards the end of the chapter—has similarities with wholesaling, in that space is purchased at favourable terms and resold to shippers who cannot meet the conditions to qualify for the lower rates.

Yet another type of outlet is formed by the sales offices of other airlines; this is the highly developed and effective special feature of the airline business—interline selling.

Although all airlines naturally do their best to attract passenger and cargo business to their own systems, they will frequently find that requests will be received for journeys and cargo movements to places they do not serve, but which they can satisfy by junctioning, at some point in their network, with another airline which does operate to the required destination. The growth of world air traffic has led to such developments in this type of business, that airlines not only concern themselves with using interline connections in order to avoid turning away customer enquiries they receive, but court other airlines who have interline traffic on offer, or who can give them access to destinations in strong demand.

IATA is most often exposed to public view in its price-fixing capacity. As one of its many less noticed but highly valuable functions, it has developed remarkable world-wide machinery to ease this interline movement. Starting with standardised documentation as a pre-requisite, there exists a series of multilateral interline agreements to cover passengers, baggage and cargo, the effect of which is that all member airlines joining the agreements accept each other's tickets and consignment notes, indemnify each other in the process, and effect settlements through a clearing house. Since fares and rates from any point in the world to any other are either specified, or can be constructed by means of agreed rules, it is possible for a passenger to pay for tickets covering a most complex world-wide journey (side-trips and all) before leaving. The originating airline will, of course, need to signal forward for onward reservations as required, and here again IATA code systems ease the way. If the passenger changes his mind *en route*, he can arrange re-routeing at any point of his journey, using his unused ticket as a cheque for the new itinerary and paying, or receiving credit for, any balance required to meet the new fare. (In fact, he may easily achieve the change at the through fare already paid.)

The tremendous scope and marketing implications of this process are demonstrated by the fact that in 1964 nearly $2,500 million arising from interline accounting were settled through the Clearing House, and that interline traffic represented as much as 40 per cent of the total business of some airlines.[1]

Looking now at the management aspects of sales outlets, the first point to be made is that this is the area where selling occurs. All that has gone before in the marketing process, as described in previous chapters, reaches its culmination when the prospective customer materialises physically, as a disembodied voice on the telephone, or as a name on a letter or telegram. He may come completely pre-sold, knowing exactly what he wants and anxious to spend the minimum amount of time securing it. He may be an enquiry, ranging from the tentative to the almost positive. Or he may be quite clear in his requirement but find he cannot have it—for example, all seats are taken on the service he wants to use.

In a sense one can differentiate between the task of selling passenger and cargo space at the outlets, mainly because a far greater proportion of cargo comes into the category of knowing exactly what it wants, than is the case with passengers. Also, contact at the point of sale between the cargo shipper and the airline is frequently not merely enquiry or booking, but reception as well, so that the same building and staff (usually still at airports) that handle enquiries and are used to effect bookings, are also receiving the cargo. Even the enquiries are much more 'professional', in the sense that the prospective shipper usually knows a good deal about the whole subject of freight movement, and can only be dealt with on the basis of factual dialogue.

The result of this is that many freight offices are untidy and battered, and the staff matter-of-fact and quite unconscious that there is any sales content in their job at all.

Whilst accepting that a different approach is necessary by the cargo sales clerk, all the requirements that exist for a passenger sales office and its personnel are required on the cargo side.

What are these requirements? They are not difficult to define; the real problem lies in finding the compromise away from the ideal which is acceptable both in terms of cost and service offered.

Firstly, the offices themselves must be well situated. This normally means, in the case of a passenger office, a site where both the resident population ('resident' here may mean resident during working hours) and the passers-by are considerable in numbers. The amount of casual business that may be attracted or lost by a difference in location of, literally, a few yards, can be considerable. For this reason, in main city centres, travel offices and particularly airline and shipping offices are found cheek by jowl in the area which is thought to offer the maximum advantages in this respect.

[1] Figures quoted from a paper entitled 'The Commercial Aspects of Airline Co-operation' by V. de Boursac, Secretary of IATA Traffic Conference No. 2.

Obviously at this point the office is in the high rental belt, and in an area where 'shop-front' design is taken seriously. Airlines, to whom design is of importance in so many fields, naturally tend to extend their expertise in this respect to their offices. Attractiveness in façade, décor, lighting, etc., automatically follows. Apart from anything else, an office which projects well in all these respects helps in its own way to support the message which prestige advertising is disseminating.

Inside the office, apart from the aesthetic aspects, functional considerations require considerable thought both as to layout and equipment.

Short-haul and long-haul requirements in this respect are not precisely the same. A good deal of short-haul business is of the straightforward 'there and back' nature, with the intending passenger clear in his mind regarding what he wants as to destination and date. It can, therefore, be handled very much like any other fairly straightforward shop transaction, with counters at which the customers stand. Indeed, because short-haul transactions, by their very nature, bring in less money per journey and the *booking* cost is little or no less whether it be for a London–Paris or Tokyo–New York reservation, it frankly does not pay to encourage the passenger to settle down for a long chat about his plans.

Though some long-haul journeys may also be simple and straightforward, it is much more characteristic for these bookings to have added complications. Long-haul offices, therefore, are often furnished with desks rather than counters, with chairs for the customers. There is a little more to this, of course, than pure functionalism. The customer is spending one or more hundreds of pounds or thousands of dollars, and any business in that bracket of individual sale will be very unwise to give its clientèle the impression that there is any hurry, however efficiently or politely the whole transaction is managed. The psychology of large purchases, to coin a pseudo-scientific phrase, calls for a slowing down of all the processes at the moment of truth when the sale is being consummated!

The airlines, individually, have exercised considerable ingenuity in building into the design of the working side of the counter or desk all the experience they have accumulated in their years of development. Each clerk's position needs to be equipped with telephone, plus any other devices (dependent on the system) connecting him with the reservations office. Appropriate reference timetables, information manuals, etc., must be immediately to hand, as well as supplies of literature, etc., that may be needed for handing over to passengers or enquirers. Probably there will also have to be security arrangements for ticket stock and cash, though frequently the actual payments have to be made to a cashier at another counter. All airlines will vary somewhat in their systems so that generalisation is not possible. Whatever the variations, well thought out equipment for the counter-clerk will enable time to be saved for both customer and clerk, and reduce error.

Intending or potential customers, whether for passenger tickets or cargo space, will call, telephone, write, or even telegraph. They will not neatly space out their several approaches to the airline in such a way that their requests spread evenly during the traditional working day. Therefore the number of counter units and public telephones, and the staff that man them, together with the number of clerks in the correspondence section, ideally are adequate to meet the peak demand by period and time of day, without any delay to the intending purchaser. And like every other aspect of the airline business the ideal, from the service point of view, is only attainable at a cost which by any standards of judgment is unacceptable. Moreover, at times of minimum demand, as in the middle of the night or during public holidays, it must be possible for people to effect a booking, simply because urgent travel requirements do arise at these times. The airline should never be 'closed' or thought to be so. Which is why a notice in an airline sales office window:

'Office hours 8.0 a.m. to 6.0 p.m. At other times phone. . . .' is better than:

'Office hours 8.0 a.m. to 6.0 p.m. When closed, phone. . . .'

Whilst, of course, the final solution has to be a compromise, this is a field in which too firm an endeavour to spread the load and utilise staff and equipment fully, by imposing long queues at counters, telephones and in correspondence booking sections at peak times and seasons, will react seriously on sales. All airlines, at some period or another, find themselves under pressure. In the United Kingdom, for example, the big rush to book up summer holidays begins immediately after Christmas. In so far as this pattern is reflected throughout the immediately competitive field, little actual traffic may be lost. Even so, the form of travel which would be less popular at times when a booking is easy, may very well at other times get a spill-over from exasperated customers of a highly popular airline whose offices and telephones are jammed, and whose replies to letters are a fortnight in arrears.

Such a situation is one of the most frustrating that the marketing side can face. Behind it lies the whole complicated and expensive marketing process which has brought a willing buyer to the point of sale, and there he stops and turns away. The judgment must, therefore, be made in terms of this total marketing effort that is being frustrated, rather than on the basis of concern that clerks and telephones are relatively idle at certain times. The sensible compromise *must* lean heavily in the direction of over-provision of facilities to enable the customer to make his purchase, rather than in the opposite direction.

The concentration in this chapter so far has been on the physical aspects of adequacy. But the men and women who are behind the counters, at the receiving end of the telephone, or opening the correspondence, are the real key to success or failure. This is where the sale is made or lost. This is where salesmanship, pure and simple, takes over.

Selling is a much maligned exercise, probably because so many people have been exposed to what is often called high pressure salesmanship, and have made purchases they have regretted; indeed, they often know they are going to regret it even as they allow their resistance to be eroded by the salesman. Yet the same people frequently want to be assisted in their purchasing. An unhelpful shop assistant will cause people not only to go away empty-handed but also to stay away. Helpfulness effects sales and brings people back. And this is a basic kind of salesmanship.

There is little doubt that the worst excesses—and this is not too strong a word—arise in fields where the sale is very much in the 'one-off' category, that is to say in sales of items which last years or a life-time. The threat never to deal with the firm again is empty in the circumstances. But an organisation which markets goods or services requiring repeat orders to stay in business, simply cannot afford selling methods which leave the customers irritated at those methods, even if not too unhappy about the purchase. Airlines are very much in a 'repeat-order' business and, moreover, look to a great part of their sales development from word-of-mouth recommendation of satisfied clients. They simply cannot afford to over-sell their product.

The counter and telephone staff of an airline are its ultimate sales people who, however adequately they are supervised and monitored, will, individually, make more or less sales during any working day dependent on two basic characteristics—their knowledge of the airline's products and their selling ability. To achieve the highest possible standards in both respects, a comprehensive and continuous training programme is essential.

Product knowledge in particular has to be genuinely continuous, in that after the new entrant has been given the basic instruction necessary before being exposed to public enquiries, all developments (schedule and price changes, new aircraft types, etc.), have to be fed in a concise, easily assimilated manner. And because nobody can remember all details, up-to-date easy reference manuals must be provided. Easy access storage of this information is one of the design aspects of the counter and telephone clerk's desk.

Training in selling techniques is only continuous in the sense that, given adequate initial training and supervision of the type that 'trains as it goes', occasional refresher courses will almost certainly be worth while, if only for the re-stimulation they always give to good staff.

It is very likely that the airline will need to operate its own training courses for both aspects—product knowledge and salesmanship. Commercial courses in salesmanship, which exist in profusion in most developed countries, vary enormously in efficiency. Only a fairly large firm can afford its own sales training establishment, because the number of sales staff has to be substantial to utilise, over the year, a permanent training organisation. But even the smallest firm, by hypothesis, needs its salesmen to be able to sell as it needs its secretaries to be able to type!

The discovery that there are techniques of selling to be learned is fairly recent, particularly in countries like Great Britain that sold for years on product advantages—even product monopolies—that have been eroded by time. Today even outstanding product advantages have to be demonstrated, which is an aspect of salesmanship. Customers have to be sought and retained; they no longer obediently come to a traditional source of supply. In these conditions, as the manager of one sales training establishment put it, you have to try really hard to make a failure of a sales training business. In such circumstances, both the excellent and the not so good tend to flourish.

But even the first class commercial sales training schools of necessity concentrate on the field of greatest demand, which is basically for the training of travelling salesmen in a variety of commodities, mainly of a standard type. Much of their training is of real value to the airline outside representative, different though his task is in many ways, particularly in the general aspects of behaviour, approach and presentation. But for the airline counter or telephone sales clerk, a good deal of this teaching is irrelevant to the task.

These differences can best be seen by looking a little closer at the typical sale in both cases. The commodity salesman is trying to convince the customer (who may be reluctant) to buy in quantity, either as retailer or user, items from his range. The airline salesman *typically* is approached by the customer for one or a few journeys or one cargo movement, either with the requirement firm ('two seats to Ruritanograd on the 1130 on the fourth') or vague ('We thought of going somewhere sunny for our holiday'). The first is easy, and would only be worth the most elementary training in politeness, if it were not for the fact that the 1130 on the fourth is sometimes full. It is easy to see that the answer 'Sorry, no seats on that' is inviting a non-sale. The first elements of salesmanship come in when alternatives, as near the time or date as possible, are offered quickly and pleasantly. There is no point in taking this process too far (high-pressure) as the passenger, on reflection, will merely cancel.

The sale simply comes unstuck if the passenger, away from the hypnotic salesman, changes his mind and cancels. Moreover, he won't expose himself to the same embarrassment next time he wants to travel. But it goes further. If he is persuaded to undertake, say, an indirect journey, at considerable inconvenience, only to discover later that a *much* more convenient direct flight was available by another airline, he will again take his future custom elsewhere. This is particularly the case with cargo shippers, who will not be happy if their consignment is held up for twenty-four hours or more awaiting a flight by the airline that has accepted it, when it could have moved much earlier by another carrier.

So the 'unsale' as a sound sales technique is important. There are times when the right thing to do, not only in the interests of customers (obviously) but also in the interests of the airline (less obviously) is to book the passengers or forward the freight by another airline. The immediate sale may be lost (though if the booking is direct a commission will be earned) but the customer is not; he is much more likely to continue to offer the booking airline his custom than if he feels he has been misled, *and* his word-of-mouth recommendation to friends and acquaintances becomes very positive instead of negative. Of course, inter-airline co-operative commercial agreements make it much easier to operate this way, but the fact does remain that, even in the harshest of competitive environments, there will be occasions when the unsale is the best sales response to an enquiry.

Although a major airline may have large numbers of sales staff in the main centres it serves, it is likely to have many others scattered round the world in relatively small groups. It is worth bringing them in for basic training. Travel costs nothing and duplicate staff will only be necessary to a minor degree, since the disadvantage of peak booking patterns can be turned to advantage by concentrating a great deal of such training in slack booking periods. Nevertheless, incidental costs of accommodation and meals for the staff brought in from distant points for such courses will not be inconsiderable.

It probably still pays, in the long run, to ensure that all sales staff are exposed to expert centralised training at least once, and fairly early, in their careers. However, if all supervisory staff are, without exception, well trained and re-trained, they can carry out a good deal of instruction in their localities. For this purpose the central training establishment should devise patterns (but not primers) of instruction which the supervisors can adapt to their local circumstances.

All large organisations, whether airlines or any other industry, with efficient and successful sales training schemes will suffer constant losses as good staff are tempted away by smaller concerns. It often pays a small concern to offer wages or salaries above the market rate for fully trained staff, rather than face the expense of uncertainty (the failure percentage) of using commercial schools for its own raw new

H

entrants. So far as small airlines are concerned, as was said earlier, there is in any case no adequate purchasable training for sales clerks.

This simply has to be accepted, and is one reason why the turn-over rate of this type of staff is usually much higher than in similar grades of employee in other parts of the organisation (for example, accounts clerks).

The features that are important at the points of sale operated by the airline itself are equally important at the points of sale operated by its agents. Reference was made earlier to the difficulty of justifying airline sales offices other than at on-line points. Elsewhere airlines are dependent on their agents, who are able to maintain offices because they book for all airlines, and almost certainly for railways and shipping companies as well.

The following figures put the relative coverage by airline sales offices and agents' offices in perspective. In the United Kingdom, its home base, British European Airways has thirty-three passenger sales offices against some 1250 agents' offices authorised to sell its international and domestic routes. Other countries and airlines may show somewhat different proportions, but the broad relationship is typical. The network of passenger and cargo agencies is a dominant part of the airlines' point of sale organisation. This is also reflected in the proportion of business sold through agents. This does vary considerably as between airlines and is invariably higher for international travel than for domestic travel. But a not untypical example is the two-thirds and more of British European Airways' international passenger business that is booked through the travel agents.

It is worth noting that the agent is in a particularly favourable position to attract bookings. Few passengers or cargo shippers merely want the journey, particularly internationally. Passengers will want hotel accommodation, passports, currency and, perhaps, side excursions, and so far the airlines have not set themselves up generally to offer these facilities.

The tendency to use the agent is not confined to holiday-makers. Many businesses with heavy travel commitments use an agency in preference to having their own self-controlled travel department. It costs them less, because the agent is remunerated by the commissions he gets from the transport organisations and hotels. Cargo shippers in turn will want customs clearance and other formalities. Although the airlines do offer some of these basic services, on the whole the relatively few large international cargo forwarding agents, who tend to dominate the scene, still provide a more complete over-all service than most, if not all, airlines.

In all these circumstances, airlines have to accept that a large amount of the business they attract will make contact with a point of sale which also sells its competitors (air and surface), and may employ staff less well-trained than they would like.

The result of all this, of course, is that a great deal of airline marketing activity centres round the passenger and cargo sales agent.

To begin with, so far as international movement is concerned, the IATA members have built up a body of agency rules and may only pay commission to agents who are appointed within these rules. They are designed to work three ways; firstly, to ensure that only well-founded agents, with good premises, expert staff, etc., receive appointments; secondly, to protect the airlines against losses by rigidly applied regulations as to the dates by which agents shall pay the money due to their principals; and thirdly, by fixing maximum rates of commission and controlling gifts etc., to agents, to guard against a rat-race of airlines buying traffic from the agents by out-bribing each other.

Within this framework, airline agency men seek to build up good-will with their agents, work to place their individual publicity on the walls and in the display windows and their leaflets on the counters, keep the sales clerks up-to-date with information, and generally find every way they can (within the rules) of inducing the agent to sell their airline in preference to the competitor's. The net result is that a well situated and creative agency is almost overwhelmed by sales calls and masses of publicity and information material. All this will cover every aspect of the airline that is needed by the agent but he will, in the end, use the manual that suits him best, for the IATA system being what it is, the fares and rates and complicated tariff provisions are the same for all airlines. Indeed, when it is realised that a large agency at a busy international centre can represent twenty or more airlines, it will be seen that the multiple aspects of IATA standardisation alone make it possible for an agent to handle business efficiently, on behalf of so many different principals, without delay and a high rate of error.

This proliferation of promotion all looks very wasteful and perhaps it is. It is, however, not exceptional. Concentrated effort on retailers by consumer goods firms is characterised by the same large amount of expenditure which produces no result. It could be argued that here we are in the area of combativeness which some economists regard as wasteful, because costs are raised unnecessarily. On the other hand it can also be argued that this is a price that developed societies pay for the choice which is available to them. Only one thing is certain— as things are, the airline that opts right out of this battle (for such it is in many respects) at the agency point of sale, will not get much traffic from this vital source.

The major operator from a particular centre will always have certain advantages in the agency field. Firstly, if an airline is large enough to run sales training courses for its own staff, it can extend these to include specially devised training courses for agency staff. Secondly, it has more opportunity to offer 'experience flights' to agency personnel—a pleasant and memory-stimulating method of inculcating product knowledge and much more effective than the best written description! Lastly, it is likely to have greater frequency of operation. It is an old adage in the airline business that if an airline operates to point A every day, one big advantage it has over a competitor that operates three times a week is that the agency staff do not have to remember the days of operation.

In the long run, the operator that offers the best reservation service will probably have an advantage over all the others, and this aspect will be elaborated in the next chapter.

Perhaps the most interesting and final point to make on the agency question is what emerges when an airline test-calls its agents. Apart from any knowledge the airline acquires about the efficiency of particular agency staff on the one hand, and its own information services on the other, it usually finds that the main concern of the well informed, professionally competent agent is to assist the caller to make the choice which most suits his needs!

In these circumstances it is tempting to think in terms of merchandising—selling 'through' the agent by advertising and point of sale display material. In a sense this is attempted, as all the advertising is designed to send the customer to the agent pre-sold on the airline, and the point of sale material is there to keep him sold when he arrives. If he positively asks for XYZ airlines by time and date he will be sold just that. But if there is any uncertainty, even as to timings, or if the first choice is full, the agent will offer alternatives to suit the expressed need—including, of course, any expressed preference for a particular airline. The simple merchandising methods open to the consumer goods industries, particularly via self-service outlets, are not effective in the airline business merely because of the impossibility of concentrating on a standard, advertised, display product which can be picked up and dropped in the shopping bag on the way round the stores.

Although airlines are free to make their own arrangements for domestic agencies, that is, agencies exclusively booking domestic services (apart from any national legislation on the point), the tendency is to appoint all IATA agents as domestic agencies also (for obvious reasons), and *not* to have an extensive additional body of purely domestic agencies. Obviously, if the IATA agency network is widespread, there is no point in adding to the administrative burden and cost of having a secondary network of agencies with limited earning potential.

Although this system is effective it can be criticised for its inflexibility. For example, agencies will only get their IATA licence if they are capable of handling the most complicated of bookings. Yet it can be argued that, since a great deal of travel is simply 'out and back', it might be more productive to have less sophisticated requirements, with lower commission rates, for agencies licensed only for the simple tasks, restricting the full licences to the highly professional all-purpose agencies who would be rewarded accordingly. The 'simple' category could then, perhaps, be approved and cancelled to meet marketing needs by local processes of a less elaborate character than those required for a full IATA licence.

In Chapter III the point was made that the actual transport is not wanted of itself, and earlier in this chapter an advantage the agent has over the airline sales office in attracting custom, was seen to be the wider service he offers. So far as the purely holiday market is concerned, therefore, the agent has always tended to find many of his customers requiring travel *and* accommodation at destination as a minimum. A natural development, particularly as a means of overcoming sales resistance to the problems of holidaying in foreign languages and currencies, was for the agent to put together the complete holiday—travel, accommodation, excursions etc.—with agency staff at transfer points *and* at destination to eliminate the language problem. The package would then be marketed at an inclusive price, paid in advance in the currency of the purchaser.

The inclusive holiday—often described by the older and misleading term 'inclusive tour'—ante-dates not only the airline but the aeroplane by many decades. The airlines in Europe made their bid to get into this business quite early (in the 1930's), by offering agents extra commissions on fares when tied in with inclusive holidays, thus giving the agent an incentive to develop this particular type of market. Today the airlines often go further and offer special low fares (ITX fares), which are only usable for this purpose (see Chapter VI).

At this point the agent moves from merely being an agent of airline and hotel in an *ad hoc* way, to being a tour operator, often taking the hotel rooms on block reservations and seeking to do the same with the airline. As his business grows he may well find it pays him to take the risk of chartering whole aircraft which operate, say, a fortnightly run out and back, 'connecting' with a block of hotel rooms. The aircraft that takes 100 holiday-makers outwards, takes back the 100 holiday-makers who have just vacated the 100 rooms that are continuously occupied by this process. Of course, any failure to sell the whole aircraft and block hotel allocation at any time during the season, reduces revenue with no reduction in cost, whereas the purely agency sale of an airline ticket has a standard commission and no risk to the agent. The tour operator has ceased to be an agent, and is a retailer of something he has manufactured from components he has purchased.

An inclusive holiday based on scheduled airline seats and ITX fares does not have quite the same characteristics, because the tour operator does not buy a block of seats and take the risk of not selling them. He has his risk in the hotel block booking, but the airline continues to carry the risk of its seats on offer being sold or not up to the moment of flight. But, if the airline is filling well, the agent then has another risk, that of being unable to get an airline seat to match the booking he has got for an empty hotel room.

Therefore, once the agent has built up a heavy flow of business to a popular resort, the risks of charter are worth taking. Normally he can make more profit if his holiday sells near to capacity, and he has the whole co-ordinated operation much more under his control. The bulk ITX contracts introduced in 1965 on some routes in Europe by some scheduled airlines, are designed to meet the competition of the charter by offering blocks of seats firmly available and *paid for in advance*, so that the financial risk goes now to the tour operator.

In recent years, in strong markets for international holiday travel, the situation has arisen where large tour operators have developed who are specialists in their field, and are no longer travel agents selling individual tickets and putting together inclusive holidays. They are, in fact, principals in their own right, using the established agency network to sell their total product on an over-all commission basis. From the point of view of the airline whose services are included in such packages, the tour operator represents a point of sale which is quite different from that of the agent.

This development presents the airlines with very considerable problems in selling their own scheduled services in the various holiday purchasing markets they serve.

Because of the greater profits available for the (financial) risk-bearing implications of chartering, together with the administrative advantages in marrying a chartered aircraft of a given size to block-booked hotel space, the really important tour operators concentrate overwhelmingly on chartered aircraft. Even if the scheduled airline, directly or through a subsidiary, enters the charter market thus available, this still leaves the problem of the scheduled services which are supported by a smaller and smaller proportion of the holiday market for air travel.

But there is a further marketing problem in the growth of inclusive holidays marketed by tour operators. Even if scheduled airlines are used, because there is no *need* for the operator to concentrate on one airline, as all fares are the same, and because there is a booking insurance in including all who operate to the point advertised, the identity and product differentiation that the airline has been at pains and great cost to establish, is submerged. The holiday booklet is the XYZ tour operator's booklet, with minimum and equal emphasis on each scheduled airline included. Worse still, if, as is common, the booklet also includes holidays by charter aircraft, for good economic reasons these are featured much more strongly *and* show up, in this highly price-conscious market, as cheaper than the holidays using the scheduled airlines. The latter now have the minimum of marketing impact in the holiday field, where charter is the real growth point of air travel, as the graph for an important market demonstrates. (Fig. 3.)

The result of these developments at the point of sale is that the traditional method of attacking the holiday market, whereby the travel agent was encouraged by extra commissions or special ITX fares to construct inclusive holidays and become a tour operator 'on

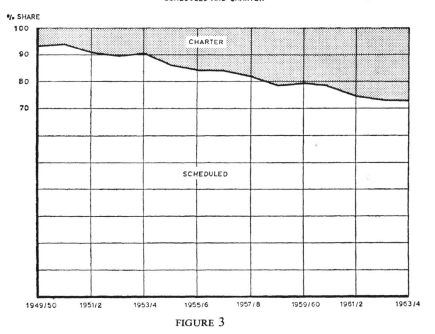

SHARES OF TOTAL AIR TRAFFIC BETWEEN UK & CONTINENTAL EUROPE

SCHEDULED AND CHARTER

FIGURE 3

the side', is currently under review. Today, the effort by the airlines to stay in the market takes various forms. Mention has already been made of the very recently introduced bulk ITX fares in Europe, which are, in effect, charters of *part* of a scheduled service to a tour operator but at a *per capita* price. This is designed to keep the traffic on the scheduled services. Another approach, which accepts the logic of the full aircraft charter to popular resorts, is for the scheduled airline to operate charters itself, or set up a fully-owned charter subsidiary, to which it often transfers its obsolescent aircraft. This subsidiary then enters the inclusive holiday charter market, in a sense in competition with its parent.

The transatlantic carriers, mainly because of United States legal restrictions, operate numerous charters in their own name for affinity groups (that is, *not* groups brought together by tour operators by advertisement). The other mass centre of tourism, intra-Europe, is typified by the wholly-owned subsidiary. A third method is for the scheduled airline to offer its own packaged holidays, usually in association with existing tour operators. These may be more expensive than the holidays using charters which are on the market, but they are built round the name and prestige of the scheduled airline.

At this relatively early stage in the battle for the holiday market between the scheduled and non-scheduled air operators, it is difficult to forecast in what form marketing policies and methods will crystallise. Certainly the charters are gaining ground rapidly. There is every reason to believe, as traffic grows, that the logic of combining aircraft and holiday accommodation into a package, all components of which are fully under the control of the organiser, must imply a continuing strong demand for charters. It is also difficult to see how a scheduled airline, selling individual seats, can offer costs comparable with a well organised and well utilised charter fleet.

One would expect, therefore, scheduled airlines either to abandon this developing mass market, concentrating on business travel and the higher priced leisure and personal travel or—much more probably —develop a fares system designed to bite as far into the holiday market as is economically possible *and* enter the cheapest end with charters. The method of entering the charter market will depend on individual assessments of the advantages and disadvantages of separate organisations and, of course, local legal or regulatory situations which may touch on this issue.

The future of the airline sponsored inclusive holiday is also a matter of speculation. Here again laws or regulations in particular countries will affect the outcome. Moreover, as travel agents as a whole dislike the entry of the airlines into what they consider their preserve, and airlines individually have spent much time and money building up agency good-will, this factor alone inhibits many airlines from moving quickly—or even at all—in this direction. But one development is probable, at least. The airline that, by whatever method, stays in the developing mass holiday market will almost certainly insist on moving from the near-anonymity, which conceals its part in the inclusive holidays advertised by many tour operators, to a dominant position in the advertising, for all the reasons enumerated throughout Chapter IX.

As a final comment on this development, one would also expect the IATA regulatory machinery to undergo changes. Major tour operators are appearing who no longer fit the pattern of agents with IATA approval who also organise packaged holidays. These businesses have no interest in individual airline bookings, require no offices open to the public, and need staff with a quite different expertise. The implications of agreed fares lead inevitably to considerations of what can be given for the fare, and in this case the tour operator is really a customer, buying airline space as part of the combined package that he markets. The regulations agreed by the IATA airlines to cover their dealings with agents and normal customers cannot be expected to fit their relationships with firms that are component purchasers.

The cargo situation at (or perhaps behind) the agency point of sale also has complications. These arise from the nature of cargo rating systems which give a rebate for quantity (see Chapter VI). If a cargo agent receives from a number of clients goods for shipment to the same point, he may find that whilst individual consignments offered direct to the airline would attract a particular level of rate, when grouped, or consolidated, they pass above a weight break-point in the tariff and qualify for a lower rate. But if the consignments come forward individually documented by the consignors to their particular consignees, the agency relationship to both consignor and carrier remains, and they do not form a single consignment for weight break-point purposes. Only when the agent changes his status with the carrier, and forwards the consolidated consignment as one, from himself as consignor to a given consignee (an agent of his own at the other end who will break the bulk consignment down and forward to the orginal addressees), does the reduced tariff apply.

All this would be simple enough if the agent merely increased his profit on the over-all transaction by any savings thus made, and carried out the fundamental aspect of his agency agreement with the airline, which is to charge to his customers the applicable airline freight rate.

But the savings available in the rate for the larger consignment may be such that he can offer, for customers prepared to accept any small delays arising from the consolidation process, a *lower* rate than they could get by going direct to the airline, whilst still making a satisfactory profit on the over-all transaction. As an agent, the consolidator cannot rebate rates to customers. But as the actual consignor he cannot be an agent. In effect, anybody, agent or not, can set up as a consolidator, ship at the bulk rates and charge what he likes to those who give him the small consignments which he has bulked. This is the weakness in any attempt by the IATA members to formulate rates to encourage consolidation (which is in their interests as it leads to larger average size of consignments with much reduced handling charges) and yet keep the rates situation under control.

In the United States the airlines are helped by national legislation for firms engaged in this type of enterprise, who are referred to as 'indirect carriers'. Elsewhere such control is absent, and although IATA does attempt to regulate such businesses—for which they have some sanctions, as most of them are also IATA approved cargo agents—this again is an area where satisfactory solutions have still to be found.

Finally, an aspect of considerable importance at the point of sale is ease of payment, including credit. For the reasons mentioned earlier, the airlines' credit arrangements with their own agents are strictly controlled. In dealings with each other the Clearing House system, to an extent, regulates inter-airline credit. It is true that unpaid balances between airlines can accrue, but the creditor airline can (and does) refuse to honour the debtor airline's travel documents if indebtedness goes on too long.

But, as between passenger or cargo shipper on the one side and airline or agent on the other, credit is a matter of personal arrangement. Business houses will not expect to pay cash for each transaction, and the IATA sponsored Universal Air Travel Plan is a generalised means of easing the sale for participants. It is, however, not a credit system but operates on the basis of renewable balances. Airlines and agents, therefore, usually have to make their own assessment of credit-worthiness of their major customers, and devise means of identifying representatives of such customers when these effect passenger bookings or forward cargo.

Generalised true credit systems exist in the form of the various competing credit card organisations. This system has gone much further in the United States than elsewhere, but even so the international traveller is frequently a credit card holder, used to paying his hotel and restaurant bills and for an increasing number of other purchases on credit by use of his card. As the credit card companies charge the seller for the facility of collecting his money, the international airlines have been in no hurry to adjust their commission rules to cover the use of credit cards for the purchase of airline tickets, believing that, in total, little extra air transport would be sold if they did so.

Credit at the point of sale, therefore, has not become a competitive weapon between airlines except in those parts of the world where loan capital attracts a very high rate of interest. In developed economies, credit to a customer is a mere matter of convenience and not a cheap way of raising a loan! But, even so, it is an important aspect of easing the sale, and a necessary adjunct to any modern and efficient sales office.

CHAPTER XI

DISTRIBUTION (RESERVATIONS)

Whatever a business produces, whether tangible commodity or intangible service, all the processes of production and marketing only achieve their consummation when the customer takes possession and makes his payment. So far as commodities are concerned, the normal situation is that the purchaser is physically distant from the production centre. Therefore, an essential element in the marketing process is for goods to be distributed to the point where the customer can conveniently take possession (for example, direct to his home, to a local retailer, etc.).

Although many services are also 'distributed' to meet the customer's needs, as with an office cleaning service, or a chain of acceptance points for laundry, dry-cleaning, etc., there are many other cases where the customer has to go personally to the source of the service in order to take advantage of it. Visits made to doctors' or medical specialists' establishments are examples, although the former usually practice with sufficient geographical scatter to make them as convenient to visit as the retail outlets for most commodities.

In the case of an airline, which operates from an airport in the vicinity of a population centre, the customer has to get himself or his cargo to that airport and, in the nature of things, there are not airports in every High Street. So, in the logical sense, air transport is not distributed to the customer; he has to come to the point of production to make use of it.

Nevertheless, as will be evident from what has been said earlier regarding the economic problems of air transport supply and demand, customers cannot be certain that the seat or space they want will be available if they simply report to the airport. The practice of reserving seats or cargo space has arisen naturally as a consequence, and the reservation system takes on some characteristics of the distribution of a commodity.

Although the customer actually requires transport, his prior need is for a firm title to the particular transport he wants—that is, a reservation. And in the same way that a manufacturer will suffer loss of sales if his distribution to point of sale is inadequate, so will an airline lose sales if *titles* to transport cannot be easily acquired. The importance, therefore, not only of a good coverage of sales outlets as described in the previous chapter, but also of an easy and trust-worthy means of access by the customer, or by the sales outlets, to the seats and hold space which the airline has available, is paramount. Thus, a first class reservations service is as potent a marketing weapon for an airline as an excellent distribution system is for a manu-facturer, and shares many of its characteristics.

Naturally, where there is no booking system none of this applies. At present passenger services which are not bookable are very exceptional. A fair amount of cargo is merely sent to airports to be got away as soon as possible, but cargo reservations still play an important part in cargo marketing.

Essentially, a reservations system consists of a record of the space available, for each day of operation, on every flight in the scheduled programme. When a request for a seat is received, enquiry has to be made of this record as to whether space is available. If it is, the booking can be accepted and the record must be amended. When the record shows that a particular flight is full, no further reservations are made on it. Cancellations work in reverse and consist of expung-ing that part of the record.

The record, of course, has to be more complete than a simple addition of numbers sold on a particular flight (or reductions in numbers still to be sold). Whether passenger or cargo any one of a variety of reasons, from a strike to a change in aircraft type leading to timing changes, may make it necessary for the reservations office to communicate with passengers or shippers who have made bookings. Cancellations too must be identifiable against bookings. Therefore, the passenger's or shipper's name and contact address and/or tele-phone number must go into the record.

The elemental airline can work with one reservations clerk and a blank book, with the services being entered day by day. On receipt of a reservation the clerk turns up the book and, if on that day to that point there is space, he accepts the reservation and makes the appropriate entry in the book. Of course, as soon as business grows and there are two clerks, neither can accept reservations while the other is referring to the book.

With further traffic growth, all advances in reservation systems have been designed with one end in view—to ensure that any sales office, passenger or shipper (or agent for either of the latter two), telephoning for space can get a quick and accurate answer. The air-line with an over-loaded system which cannot give this quick service will be avoided. The manufacturer who has not got his goods in place for the willing buyer, or who takes too long to supply after the order has been placed, will lose sales; the airline with a bad reservations organisation will suffer loss of sales exactly comparable to the losses which bad distribution imposes on a manufacturer. The converse is obviously true, and the development of a really rapid and reliable response to requests for bookings has become a potent overall marketing tool.

Starting with the 'one clerk, one book' method and jumping over intermediate developments, the typical modern airline passenger reservation system operates in general along the following lines:

Firstly, the reference and record book have been divided into two. The reference aspect has gone up on the wall in the shape of a 'sight board', and the record section has disappeared into a back room.

Beginning with the sight board: in the room where the telephone reservations or sales clerks work—for this is where speed is essential —one wall will have displayed on it, in some schematic form, all the services on sale and the dates of operation as far ahead as experience demonstrates is necessary. The obvious form is a grid. An example of this, as set up on the last day of January, is seen in Table 13 overleaf.

The actual style may be somewhat different from the example and will almost certainly be more complicated since it must accommodate extras, and may be required to signal changes from the printed timetable etc., but *basically* this is the form that a sight board takes.

The spaces blocked out simply indicate that the particular service does not operate on those days.

It will be seen that the days of operation are all filled with symbols: 'S' indicating that seats are available and can be sold; 'F' that the service is full, and 'A' that there may be seats but special application to the records control has to be made. But these symbols are only put into this example because the printing is in black and white. In fact, to aid quick appreciation of the position by the sales clerks *and* to minimise error, colours will be used instead, probably green for 'sell', red for 'full' and yellow for 'apply'.

Before enlarging on 'apply' it is necessary to look at the other aspect, the record section, which is the link between the sales clerk and the reference sight board.

In the original, simple, system, the man who made the reservation—after seeing that space was available—entered up the record. If he, or another clerk, received another request for the same service on the same day immediately afterwards, the record was up-dated.

The modern system, as described, gives a time-lag. The way it works is this. The clerk, having received a request and made the reservation, because his instant appraisal of the board gives him a green 'sell' indication, makes out an individual record of the booking —name, address, destination, date, flight number—probably on a specially designed card. This then goes (by continuous conveyor or

TABLE 13. *Sight Board showing seat availability, for use in a passenger reservations office*

Destination	'Service' No.	February 1	2	3	4	5	6	7	8	9	10	11	12	13	14	15	16	17	18	19	Other dates as required
A	XY42	F	A	S	A	S	—	—	F	S	S	A	S	—	—	F	S	S	S	S	
B	XY70	F	F	A	S	A	F	A	S	S	S	A	F	F	S	S	S	S	S	S	
	XY72	S	—	S	—	S	—	—	A	—	S	—	S	—	—	S	—	—	—	S	
C	XY90	F	S	A	S	F	F	F	F	S	A	S	A	A	F	S	S	S	S	A	
	XY92	F	—	—	—	S	A	A	S	—	—	—	S	F	S	S	—	—	—	S	
	XY94	S	S	S	S	S	S	S	S	S	S	S	S	S	S	S	S	S	S	S	
	XY96	A	—	—	—	F	F	A	A	—	—	—	F	A	S	S	—	—	—	S	
D	XY154	F	F	S	S	S	S	S	F	A	S	S	S	S	S	A	S	S	S	S	

Other services
as required.

some similar labour-saving method) to the record section. They maintain complete records of each flight in some refined variation of the original book and, on receipt of each card, they up-date this and then file the card for reference. This is important if only because of queries that arise on bookings, including queries after the flights concerned have departed.

It is obvious that, even if there is no delay in adjusting the record, with several, and perhaps very many, telephone sales clerks busily making reservations, there must be some time-lag between confirmation to the passenger and any necessary adjustment to the sight board.

If, therefore, the 'sell' indication were left until the last seat had gone, before it could be replaced by the 'full' signal further bookings might be made. To give a buffer which will obviate this, the record section will put the 'apply' sign on the board at an agreed point—say when four seats remain for sale. Any clerk wanting to sell where the signal says 'apply' must hold his telephone contact, telephone directly to the record section who, if the buffer has not been used up, will tell him to sell and they will then adjust the record simultaneously. The card that eventually reaches the record section must, of course, be clearly marked to distinguish it from one recording a 'green' sale, or there could be a double booking.

At the main traffic centres of large airlines, the situation soon arises where the size of the sight board required is impossibly large for inspection by the sales clerks, although there is a story of one airline that relied on its clerks to use field glasses to read the more remote parts of the board. Closed circuit television has been a somewhat more scientific approach to this problem. But in the end, size grows to a point where one sight board just cannot accommodate everything, and a fresh break-down on an area basis has to occur. The airline's routes are divided, for reservations purposes, into convenient 'parcels' and each has its own reservations room or hall, with appropriate sight board. All may connect with a master record section or this can, in turn, be divided. At this point two things have occurred. The telephone service has deteriorated in that all calls to the exchange have to be sorted out before going to the appropriate sales clerks. If this is overcome by each area having a separate exchange the total number of lines and chances of random saturation are increased. Similarly, the whole area concept inhibits maximum use of the labour force because it is not easy to transfer help from a slack area to a busy one.

Some airlines have introduced refinements in this basic kind of system by the use of electric or electronic devices, all designed to increase the speed of answering and accuracy of record. At best, however, they have to remain with the principle of separating selling from recording.

The greatest problem of operating an efficient reservation system, on the assumption that sufficient expertise is available to provide the most efficient service that can be justified financially, is that of human error. Even the very elementary system of 'one clerk one book' can go wrong if his entry is wrongly made, but as soon as records are copied from cards, and sight boards are adjusted from records, the chances of human error begin to multiply.

Very recently, those airlines with the largest volume of reservations have found that the more than considerable expense of computerising their reservations has been worth while (including the cost of duplication of basic equipment, since breakdown is unthinkable).

The essence of a computer is its ability to store information and make it accessible again at lightning speed. The design of suitable equipment to adapt this to the reservation problem, and the programming necessary to achieve the required results, have called for highly detailed and technical liaison between reservations specialists and computer manufacturers. The end result is to get back to the point where all sales clerks can book and record instantaneously all flights—however many there may be—and enormously reduce the possibility of human error.

At the core of the system is the computer's 'memory', acting exactly in the same way as the record system which it replaces. Each sales clerk has a 'desk set' connected with the memory. This desk set, probably by means of push-buttons, can ask if there is space and will relay the answer in the form (usually) of lights on a small panel which is part of the individual desk set. If this is positive (sell), another push-button operation records the sale instantly in the memory, thus up-dating the record. Devices can be built in so that alternatives are offered if the flight is full, and other devices which warn or inhibit the clerk if he makes mistakes, so further obviating the possibility of human error.

Remembering that the object throughout is to make it quick, easy and inexpensive for customers and agents to effect reservations, the computer offers a further advantage over conventional systems. Any system works less adequately in these respects, the further the enquiry is removed from the reservations record. Although telephone efficiency varies immensely in different countries, and in some areas long distance calls are now as simple and rapid as local calls, they do get more costly with distance. With the computer there is no problem (at a cost) of having desk sets, hundreds of miles away, connected direct to the system, acting in every respect as speedily and efficiently as those in the same building.

Incidentally, it is obvious that there is no problem, whatever system is used, in having the people who receive booking requests by post or wire married into the system. In both cases there is somewhat less urgency; it is the enquirer on the telephone whose requirement for speed of reply dominates the whole organisation.

All that has been detailed up to now relates to a system of simple on-line one sector request. We have been looking at the problems of offering a good reservation service at point x to passengers who want to book *to* points A,B,C,D and any others to which the airline operates, and who never want to make a return booking, nor one connected onwards in some direction by the airline they are calling or by some quite different airline. In fact, passengers will want return and onward reservations.

And again, demand will arise thousands of miles away for the services operating from point x on an interline basis, in connection with airlines feeding *into* x. It may be said that all this complicates the situation enormously, as it does, but here again, the simplest facts of marketing life indicate that the airline which can most effectively offer this service will get the traffic.

Take first the simple case of the return booking, requested in connection with the outward booking and, indeed, an essential part of the whole transaction. People on holiday, in particular, are disinclined to buy a return ticket unless reservations both ways are firmed up as part of their over-all holiday plan. In the earlier days a complicated system was adopted of allocating to each point a certain number of seats for return journeys. Of course, these had to be based on averages and the result was always a stream of demands to the distant points for extra reservations and for reservations to be released from the allocation, as well as messages covering release of unsold space back to the point of origin.

In the case of places where demand for space out of point x is heavy, the central reservations office allows them to sell (and report what they have done, of course), without reference to the record until they receive a 'stop-sale' message. In other words, for the particular demands that arise at such a distant point, the central office is in effect giving them a perpetual green until the warning message is received. This puts such places very nearly in the same position as point x itself, and enables very easy and rapid selling to take place against all requests for which there is space. Indeed, where communications are good, the system that tends to emerge is a central space control holding *all* space in and out, with the peripheral stations selling and reporting in the manner described. Naturally, this makes the time-lag between sale and up-dating of the record even longer, and so buffers have to be adjusted accordingly.

The introduction of a central computer, with the ability to 'remote' its tentacles and yet lose nothing of the advantages of instantaneous reaction between sale and up-dating of the record, makes the central space control concept even more obviously right.

I

All these developments can lead to a situation where any station in the network, and indeed the agents within each station's area, can make reservations, however complicated, embracing journeys confined to the sectors operated by the airline, with speed and accuracy. But many requests will need to be made to other airlines for onward space where interline journeys are being arranged, and the reservations system must also cope quickly and efficiently with requests *from* other airlines as part of their interline selling.

Methods used for this kind of reservation vary from the unbelievably primitive to the highly sophisticated, and the hard fact is that a sales clerk will do his utmost to persuade a customer *not* to continue a journey by an airline which has a time-consuming and/or erratic interline booking service.

Apart from such obvious improvements (over individual written or telegraphed requests) as allowing sub-offices in areas of heavy interline demand to work on 'sell and report', or having private lines to other companies' local offices linked with their own centralised reservation systems, one of the more interesting sales methods is free sale. The airline using this invites other airlines to book freely up to no more than, probably, two seats at a time, and report them up to a specified period (say seven days) before the date of flight. They never receive any stop-sale messages. The airline adopting this system, as an attractive way of improving interline sales, again has to have a buffer of seats to absorb these reservations as they come in.

The really interesting development in this field so far as the computer is concerned is that, when two airlines both have computers, they can be connected together so that, in effect, the computers are 'talking' to each other.

All these pre-computer developments have one aim in common, easement of the sale. The price paid for this is a loss of accuracy. And errors work in two directions: on the one hand against the airline itself when passengers do not arrive for seats held for them, and on the other when passengers arrive and find no seats available for them. The revenue loss inherent in the first case can be deliberately accepted as a cost of the system. The good-will loss that may occur in the second is much more serious and difficult to evaluate.

Of course, every error of this kind is not disastrous. Firstly, some 'no-show' passengers may conveniently leave seats available for the over-bookings, and secondly over-bookings may (and usually do by the nature of things) occur on flights which are not fully sold, so that fortuitously space is available anyway. So that the problem, in the end, is not the over-booking as such but the over-sale.

It is quite impossible to devise a reservations system that will protect the airline completely from the possibility of over-sales, simply because any system is subject to human error. However, airlines using methods to ease sales, such as have been described, are obviously more prone to over-sales than those with more primitive systems. But the public at large, and the agents who are booking on their behalf, must not only find the reservations system easy and quick to use, they must also find it reliable on so high a proportion of occasions that the rare over-sale is statistically acceptable. And there is really no more to say than that about the limits to which any airline can go in developing sell and record and, particularly, free sale techniques.

All this detail relates to passenger reservations systems. Apart from the fact that cargo reservations systems do not have to cope with the return reservation, quite simple recording methods can generally be used. The methods are unimportant—the principles remain the same. The shipper who wants to send his freight on a particular day must have a quick and reliable answer. But, of course, much freight really does only require 'quick service', and does not need assurance that it will go on a particular flight. The high frequency airline can, therefore, attract much freight which is un-booked and which relies (from experience) on the airline to deliver within acceptable time limits. So that the reservation by a particular flight does not dominate the position as it does in the case of passengers.

Adequate control of space, on mixed passenger/cargo aircraft, is, of course, a matter of vital economic interest to the airline, but space control is not a marketing problem as such. It is economically important to see that cargo does not shut out potential (higher-rated) passenger load. But it is also important, from the marketing point of view, to ensure that a regular flow of freight is not interrupted just so that an extra passenger can be accommodated on a particular day. Therefore, within sensible economic limits set by traffic flow experience, day-to-day space control has to be concerned with the underlying market situation.

Of necessity this chapter has had to elaborate somewhat on reservations systems as such, but it has essentially been concerned with the importance of any such systems in the over-all marketing objective.

In particular, its main purpose has been to bring out the basic problem of balancing one hundred per cent accuracy (the ideal) against ease of selling. Computerisation, if it makes economic sense in the circumstances of any particular airline, should do a great deal to reduce the possibility of inaccuracy whilst actually increasing the ability to sell quickly and positively.

But computers have only just commenced their entry into this field and are limited, because of cost, to a few of the really large operators. For many years to come most airlines will be reserving on systems which are variants in one way or another of those outlined earlier in this chapter.

The eventual success of a non-computerised reservation system in meeting the requirement of easy sale and minimal inaccuracy, is completely dependent on the quality of over-all supervision. However intelligently the buffers etc. are set, they must still be calculated on averages. An interline booking from airline x may never eventuate and no cancellation will be received; airline y is more reliable. This route books early, that one books late. A holiday route suffers little change from cancellations as it books up, a business route may suffer so many changes that the aircraft capacity is booked and cancelled several times before it departs.

Therefore, whatever the mechanics of the system, its success depends on expert supervisory staff constantly watching the booking pattern route by route and making day-to-day adjustments, periodically 'cleaning up' by checking bookings which their experience warns may be suspect and, in particular, ensuring that no flight is released to the airport consciously overbooked. If there is an overbooking for some reason, the irritation to the passenger concerned arising from a phone call offering an alternative, is nothing compared with what he experiences when he reports at the airport and is offloaded.

Although it is much more a matter of airline economics than marketing, it would be wrong to ignore the problem of the no-show in a chapter dealing with reservations.

It is perhaps a fault of the international airlines that they have not been able to agree amongst themselves on a universal system whereby the passenger, who books and does not turn up, forfeits all or part of his fare. There are, of course, many difficulties. Much travel is on credit from business houses or from other airlines. So the money is not actually in the till to be retained, if a rule applies. Because booking records can be (and sometimes are!) kept in pencil, to keep the goodwill of a big client an airline could expunge a booking record, not charge the IATA agreed amount, and so gain a competitive advantage. In any case, arguments can arise as to whether a cancellation was made and not registered, because of an error in the reservations office. Again, should 'compassion' be shown for sickness etc.? If not, people will react against the hard-faced airline; but if such reasons are accepted, this increases the opportunities of competitive evasion of the rules by unscrupulous airlines.

Domestically, where the problem of firm regulation and competitive abuse may be small or completely absent, airlines often have such company imposed regulations which they can 'bend' to meet individual cases. Internationally, the tendency is to try to overcome the no-show problem, which can be very serious, by reconfirmation procedures. This implies that, the booking having been made, it has to be re-confirmed, say forty-eight hours before date of travel or it is cancelled. Whatever merit this may have in clearing up the lists, it does not really permit time for resale and can be a burdensome and even worrying problem for the passenger.

The airlines have a long way to go before they achieve anything like a satisfactory solution to this problem. But when, as can be the case, not inconsiderable numbers of passengers on the booking list simply fail to appear, it must be obvious that the whole reservations system is not performing its part of the marketing function as efficiently as it should.

CHAPTER XII

CUSTOMER SERVICE

There is a danger, in discussing the marketing aspects of a service, of expanding the concept further and further until it embraces the whole, if only because the *way* the service is performed on each occasion has such a potent influence on its continued marketability. It is not too difficult to divide production from marketing in the abstract, but in practice it can be rather more difficult. So far as air transport is concerned, the many personal aspects which exist in the product that the customer finally enjoys, cause ostensibly production functions to spill over into the marketing field, so that one cannot really define the 'factory' in air transportation, cutting off all functions that take place outside the gates to identify firmly as 'marketing'.

The aircraft—the basic production units—have to be maintained and made available in appropriate numbers, types and places to operate the schedules formulated along the lines described in Chapter VIII. Exactly the same applies to the aircrew. There can be no doubt that the end result of all this, aeroplanes being flown in accordance with the published schedules, is the essential production process of the airline, and marketing interest is confined to all aspects being well executed.

But the passengers, their baggage, the cargo and the mail need to be received and checked, placed on the aircraft, serviced aboard (in the case of passengers mainly), removed at the other end and sent on their way. All this is what is generally called the traffic function. Is this part of production, or an element in the marketing process?

It is possible to bring some kind of logic to bear on this and argue that there is a series of functions which bring staff continually and personally in touch with the passengers or shippers, and these, therefore, have a marketing slant, whilst other functions behind the scenes imply no contact and, therefore, are genuinely part of production. On this analysis the clerk at the airport behind the reception desk who checks a passenger's ticket, assesses excess baggage charges (if any), issues a boarding card and informs the passenger where he should go next, is obviously 'marketing'. The men who take the checked baggage and load it into the aircraft are 'producing'.

But the whole complex series of processes at an airport which relate to the reception and emplaning of the load, including the reverse procedures on arrival of aircraft, are so interrelated that they must be kept within the same control. It simply would not work to have two station managers dividing up this traffic work between them, each reporting upwards in quite different departmental organisations, just to satisfy a rather specious piece of analytical organisational logic. Apart from any problems that this might pose in the ordinary day-to-day working, at times when things go wrong (weather or technical delays, changes of aircraft type necessitating load changes) authority has to be firmly vested in one man and his chain of command if action is to be taken quickly. And speedy decision followed by speedy action is essential in all such cases.

So from the marketing point of view, the important thing is that there shall be this unified control, wherever it may fall in the organisation. However, those parts of the traffic handling function which are directly concerned with the public—customer services—must be performed in a way that accepts the psychological differences between dealing with people and calculating loads in a back-room. Somewhere in the airline, arrangements have to exist for a dialogue on these matters to ensure the optimum compromise between keeping people content and the cost thereof; because if these functions are viewed too narrowly through production oriented eyes, the net result can be efficient, low in cost, but quite inhuman.

The constituents can be summarised diagrammatically, as in Table 14 overleaf.

These few basic processes are never *more* simple than this, and can be more complex. For example most airlines maintain or use air terminals in the centres of towns served by the airports they use, for those finding it inconvenient to report direct. Whether the formalities of baggage collection etc. are performed at the town terminal or at the airport, this additional process imports another holding aspect in the form of the wait for the coach taking the passenger from terminal to airport.

Therefore, quite apart from the importance of ensuring that the personal aspects of the contact between airline staff and passenger or shipper are well handled each time contact is made, there is the other feature to be considered—the effect of the periods of waiting between processes.

In the case of cargo, provided the over-all through carriage time between receipt of the consignment and its delivery is satisfactory, the cargo itself is not disturbed by periods of waiting. The airline, of course, will want to reduce the time it holds cargo at either end (for

TABLE 14. *Aircraft arrival and departure—traffic and control functions*

	PASSENGERS	FREIGHT
	Journey to the airport	Carriage to the airport
	Reception by the airline (check ticket, reservation and baggage—accept baggage)	Reception by the airline (check and perhaps complete documentation, weigh, allocate flight)
DEPARTURE	Emigration formalities (possibly including outward customs and currency control)	Outward customs clearance
	HOLD	HOLD
	Embark passengers and baggage	Load
		(occasionally) notify consignee of despatch
	Disembark and unload baggage	Unload
	Immigration	Clear customs
ARRIVAL	Customs	Either: Notify consignor and
	Hand over baggage	HOLD
	Journey from airport	HOLD until collected
		Hand over to consignor
		Deliver to consignor

straightforward economic reasons) to reduce warehousing space to the minimum. So here the airlines' urge towards economy favours the marketing requirement completely. But passengers who find themselves 'hanging around' between all the processes of embarkation and disembarkation tend to become extremely impatient, so that a departure delay coming on top of all this can produce a genuinely hostile reaction.

Of course, from every point of view, both in the case of passengers and freight, the ideal to which every good traffic man bends his mind is to achieve an uninterrupted flow through all the processes on departure and on arrival. Apart from the fact that ideals are never attainable all the time because of varying external causes, two major factors work against the airlines' endeavours. The first is the existence of governmental control embedded in the processes of international travel and carriage (domestic flights are spared these) and the second is the necessity of using airports owned by somebody other than the airline.

So far as controls are concerned, that is to say passport and customs formalities and the like, all airlines throughout the world join together in what is happily called a 'facilitation' programme, designed to bring constant pressure on States to simplify, streamline and, where possible, eradicate these controls. And there is no doubt that tremendous strides have been made from the days just after the war when every passenger and shipper was made to feel like a criminal.

Airlines, however, can never finally eliminate the problem of having their passengers (particularly) handled by people who owe no allegiance to the overriding commercial requirement of keeping the customer happy. Two customs officers may be allocated to examine the baggage of a complete aircraft load of passengers, and they have no incentive to quicken their pace in order to ease the wait of the last to be cleared. And the welcoming smile and carefree greeting is, professionally, quite the wrong approach to someone who may turn out to be a smuggler.

Turning to airports, the influence of air terminal design and layout on both efficiency and even-flow processing is enormous. If holding has to occur between processes, these are much more bearable in comfortable, spacious clean lounges than in austere, cramped and dirty surroundings. Short, well sign-posted passages from process to process are less wearing on the nerves (and feet) than the reverse.

When starting with airports which have to be taken as they are, the airlines find it necessary to work constantly with airport authorities to secure the improvements they require. Such improvements are designed not merely to improve efficiency, that is, reduce cost, but to remove every possible irritation from the necessary, but always potentially maddening surround to the *real* product that has been marketed, the actual air journey.

What has been said about airports is equally, perhaps even more, true of access to airports. Airports are in the vast majority of cases, because of the ground area required, far or even very far from town centres. Often they grow up in areas where the roads are no more than country lanes. Here again the pressure has to be maintained on the appropriate authorities to improve roads, build rail spurs, even provide public transport facilities—all of which gets a little easier each year that traffic grows and total volume becomes important. But progress in this way is essential, particularly for short-haul transport, as the whole advantage of the speed and comfort of the air journey can be utterly negated by tedious road journeys and inefficient airports at either end. The product, which has been fashioned with such care and expense to meet the marketing re-quirement, will lose a great part of its appeal if these adjuncts to the product, which are unhappily in other people's hands, are sub-standard.

To return now to something which is very largely in the control of the airline—the whole question of staff attitude. The staff in question, of course, are solely those in touch with the customers.

The importance of concentrating on this in training sales staff (counter and telephone) was noted in Chapter X, and in a sense is an elaboration of the obvious in that a pleasant and helpful manner must be more effective in selling anything, than surliness and a casual approach to the customer's requirement. But it is equally important, though frequently neglected, that these attributes are found in all the staff who handle the customers *after* they made their purchases. In a sense every one of these staff is manufacturing a part of the product specially for that customer before his very eyes. And the manner in which it is done will affect the quality of the immediate service being rendered and, in the end, contribute to (or detract from) the over-all quality of the total product.

This attitude training for non-sales staff is much more difficult than it seems. In fact, historically, it was not easy in the case of telephone sales clerks because they regarded themselves as reservations clerks. Once they accepted that their function was to sell, they became at least psychologically open to good attitude training.

A prerequisite of success is careful selection of staff to be employed on these customer-facing tasks. This at least gives the opportunity of examining new entrants critically, with customer relations aspects in mind. And while this will not prevent errors in selection, it should mean that a higher proportion are amenable to attitude training. If one defines good manners as consideration for other people, this is really all one is seeking. If staff have not got this basic attribute one can teach them a few useful aids to keeping the customer happy, such as addressing him by name; but the real requirement of the urge to help does not sink very deeply into such people. The young man or woman who really brings to the task a natural eagerness, not only to put the world right (which is common), but also to sort out the insignificant problems of one individual (which is somewhat less common), needs little or no attitude training. In fact, they may have to be told gently that they are doing splendidly, but that they must be a little more economical in the amount of time they devote to each passenger.

After selection, it is important that the introductory courses which these staff will need on the technical aspects of their jobs, are heavily impregnated throughout with attitude training. Traffic staff must be trained in many aspects of processing and loading work so that they can be interchangeable. The final fully trained man or woman may or may not be dealing with passengers or shippers. The danger then arises that the detailed training on the factual side will be just that, and attitude training will be left to a somewhat perfunctory lecture at the end (perhaps by a visiting member of the sales staff, as though it is an alien thing). The whole impression left with the trainee is that it is not very important and at best a separate 'subject' in the curriculum whereas, of course, it is the very heart of the customer handling function.

If an airline has been negligent in its attitude training, it will have a very tough battle on its hands before it sees results once it starts to try to put things right. The re-training of older men and women who have got set in casual and indifferent ways is difficult enough almost to deserve the description 'impossible'. On the other hand, once the base has been set and the staff *as a whole* are imbued with the required attitude, this serves to keep the level up because all new entrants automatically react to the atmosphere.

Finally, on this question of attitude, the only way to keep the standard high is by generous establishments in the matter of supervision. This serves two purposes. There is the obvious one of ensuring that the staff are doing their various tasks properly. But a passenger or shipper with a problem, however adequately he is being handled by a lower grade employee, immediately feels better about it all if the supervisor is readily accessible.

It may appear that this heavy emphasis on staff attitude is a little over-done, if one is merely thinking of ways and means of ameliorating the small irritations of waits between processes, or even the more important 'image of the airline' at all points. But there is another factor which strongly reinforces the whole argument for inculcating in staff the kind of attitude which has been described. Unlike purchasers of other commodities and services in general, the air traveller may be apprehensive. Some reference was made in an earlier chapter to this situation.

If one reads what the professional psychologists have written on this matter, it invariably comes down to the latent possibility, under stress of anxiety, of the whole thing breaking out in the form of verbal violence aimed at the nearest employee. This can happen at any time, for instance when a service is delayed on departure. Not only will the employee with the right attitude be able to handle such passengers better, but employees with the wrong attitude can easily *cause* it to happen.

The other aspect of customer service which is worth mentioning separately is service aboard the aircraft.

Naturally, all that has been said on other parts of customer service apply here too, and often with greater force. For example people who are apprehensive before a flight can be in a highly advanced state of anxiety once the wheels are off the ground. Also, passengers in the aircraft are exposed to the attentions of the few cabin staff for the whole flight, and not to a series of changing people as at the airport. Therefore the behaviour of the stewards and stewardesses—who in any case are *constantly* being watched by at least some of the passengers—is a matter of outstanding importance. Anyone who has flown a really long-distance journey involving, say, four changes of cabin crew *en route*, will have noticed how apparent are differences in the way each crew sets about caring for the passengers on its sector. Frequently this is simply a matter of personal variations on a general theme of excellence. But one indifferent crew immediately pin-points the importance of the contribution to passenger ease that good cabin service provides.

Further facets of the cabin service—food, drink, provision of newspapers etc., will, of course, have a very important impact on the passenger. But these are part of the product, the marketing influence on these having already been exercised through the product planning machinery in the airline (see Chapter VIII).

At the end of Chapter VII reference was made to General Sales Agency (GSA) agreements, and this is a suitable point at which to examine this particular method of area marketing.

Briefly it consists of an agreement under which an airline entrusts the whole of its local marketing in an area to another organisation, which may (but need not necessarily) be another airline. If the general sales agent *is* another airline, it will, of course, not be one that is directly competitive in the area with the appointing airline.

Arrangements such as this are normally made to get some sort of coverage in markets to which the airline does not operate, and in these cases the general sales agent does very little more than distribute promotional and advertising material to individual sales agents and other airlines, arrange any specific advertising on request and generally act as a point of recourse and enquiry in the area. The other circumstances in which a GSA is used is when an airline operates with very low frequency to or through an area. In such cases the functions of reservations and accounting with agents will also need to be undertaken on behalf of the principal.

One more case of sub-contracted work needs to be mentioned in the general context of this chapter, viz. the handling agency. Here the airport work is contracted by the principal to its agent. This may be in addition to a GSA, or the principal may do its own promotion and reservations but still employ a handling agent.

The object of all these arrangements is to save money. Regional airlines in particular often draw so little traffic from areas far removed from their sphere of operation, that even the smallest marketing organisation (one man and a secretary) could actually cost more than the total revenue derived from the area. The GSA arrangement, using perhaps the distribution machinery of an established local airline for the dissemination of promotional literature, can probably be contracted at very little cost, and is just better than making no impact in the area at all.

The 'infrequent operation' case is basically the same, because now the costs of a minimum reservation service must be met; the revenue will probably be higher, but so certainly will the expenditure.

Where operations are infrequent, the common sense of sub-contracting airport and town office handling is obvious. And it is quite possible for frequency to reach a point where a small marketing organisation is worth while, because it is continually employed, whilst the long period of unemployment, between services, of staff engaged on handling aircraft and passengers makes this part of the exercise wasteful.

It is obvious that *positive* marketing cannot be expected from a general sales agent. It is commonly accepted in the industry that a really good GSA will ensure adequate distribution of literature, deal competently with enquiries, make bookings if the principal operates in the area, and in short react in accordance with his agreement. But the very best GSA cannot be expected to act independently, that is to promote the services of the principal as a result of self-generated marketing thinking. Even on the routine work one cannot expect the staff of the GSA to display, on behalf of the principal, the positive approach to agents and the public which is really required.

When it comes to a handling agent, where staff attitude is the essence of customer servicing, the problem can be even more acute.

In general, off-line, the GSA arrangement is adequate. Even when traffic emanating from a particular off-line area builds up to a substantial amount, it may still be a satisfactory solution to appoint a GSA for the purely mechanical tasks (mainly distribution of promotional material using the GSA's established machinery), but at the same time to take over the directly promotional aspects with the principal's own locally based staff.

On-line, however, it always makes sense to abandon the GSA principle and set up shop in the operating airline's own name, just as soon as the minimum expenditure necessary ceases to be too absurdly high in relation to the potential revenue.

Whilst the same argument applies in general to handling at airports and town offices, there can be a good deal of wasted time involved if the operation is infrequent—and for this purpose, in certain circumstances, even a daily service can be infrequent.

Most marketing men would still prefer that their own airline staff handle the passengers or cargo. An irritated or distressed customer asking for the XYZ representative is always more unhappy if told there is none available. The possibility does exist, however, of employing a handling agent and, in addition, some of the principal's own staff to ensure supervision of the agent and the availability of a man in the right uniform in case of need.

CHAPTER XIII

ORGANISATION OF MARKETING IN AN AIRLINE

The marketing organisations of different airlines vary considerably. Size, of course, will affect the issue. At the lower end of the scale one may find a senior executive doubling the functions of accountant and commercial manager, whilst at the other end the problem of span of control may produce two senior executives, each responsible for parts of the marketing function, reporting directly to the Chief Executive.

Apart from size, and after one has pierced the disguise of nomenclature of posts (which can confuse to the point of misleading), differing marketing mixes can cause very wide variations in the way the several functions are emphasised or grouped. The availability or otherwise of men with particular talents and ability will also cause managements to bend organisations to get the best out of the men available. Whether in doing this they sometimes go too far and build organisations round people is not always clear. All books on management rightly condemn this practice, but this should not imply that a rigid theoretical organisation must be kept intact at all costs, whatever the qualities of those who can be fitted into the slots to bring it to life.

So one cannot say that there is an ideal organisation towards which all airlines should strive. However, there are certain principles which are of general application in any airline.

Firstly, of course, all functions must be covered.

Secondly, there must be a separation between the Head Office marketing side (which lays down policy and institutes controls), and the field force which actually carries out the local promotion and selling activities. Even here some blurring may occur for convenience. For example, the Head Office advertising organisation may do the detailed planning of all the advertising schemes and campaigns in the country of base, including placing of contracts (the home field organisation being consulted); whereas away from base the field managers may well plan in detail, within the over-all policy laid down by Head Office, and make their own contracts. But this amalgamation of Head Office and field functions has dangers if carried too far. Ideally the Head Office should restrict itself to the issue of the policy guidance and directives within which the active field marketing forces operate, and institute such controls (budgets, targets, etc.) as may be necessary; it will have difficulty in doing that *to* itself, if it takes over the home area; moreover, in advising on requirements, it should hold the balance between *all* areas, and cannot do this efficiently if it is itself an area, with its own targets.

Thirdly, the link-up between those Branches and Sections which depend closely on one another must be efficient; for example, the feed between market research and the requirement setting staff must be smooth.

Fourthly, as with any management and/or administrative organisation, the span of control at each point in the pyramid must not be too great.

Fifthly, the over-all airline organisation must cope adequately and efficiently with the necessary dialogue between marketing and production.

Because there is considerable organisational diversity between efficiently marketing airlines, this chapter will not be built round an organisation diagram, for to do so would imply that *any* efficient airline should have its marketing side worked in some recognisable variation of this pattern. And this would be untrue, even if the mode itself were the theoretically perfect framework for a particular airline's marketing task.

However, looking again at the processes which have been examined in the preceding chapters, these can be brought together into a logical order, which points the way to the necessary organisation to achieve the over-all purpose with the minimum of friction and the maximum of speed and efficiency.

1 The cycle begins with the market research function, very much as set out on page 18. The object here is to gather together all the necessary information which will enable forecasts to be made in detail of the available markets. This is the basic raw material leading to the establishment of the requirement.

2 Fares and rates shown to be desirable by this consumer research (allied with cost information and forecasts) must be introduced. Where this calls for changes, there must follow negotiation through the Traffic Conference machinery of the International Air Transport Association and, in the case of domestic services, preparation of cases for presentation to the appropriate Government regulatory agency (in the case of the United Kingdom, the Air Transport Licensing Board).

3 Any necessary approvals to operate services must be cleared through the national licensing procedure (again the Air Transport Licensing Board in the United Kingdom) and, additionally, in so far as international services are concerned, through the bilateral Government Air Services Agreements.

4 The optimum commercial requirements resulting from the above (allied with information obtained in their normal day-to-day activities by the field selling organisations) must be defined. These requirements, expressed as traffic flows at the fares and rates to be applied, are fed into the operating departments. The purpose, and the result, are to ensure that production, in the form of the programme of scheduled services, corresponds as closely as possible to the detailed market requirement, having regard to fleet, crew and cost limitations.

5 The resulting schedules may have to be cleared with other carriers operating in parallel. Such clearances are often necessary because of the way in which the Government Air Services Agreement is written. But it will *always* be necessary where there is a co-operative agreement with another airline, as the whole purpose of such agreements is to plan route capacity and marketability as a whole.

6 The final traffic flow forecasts, adjusted to the finalised programme of scheduled services, must be converted into money, giving the airline's total revenue budget for the period and this, in turn, must be divided into area targets for control purposes.

An organisational point of some importance relates to the fourth of these processes, wherein the commercial requirement as a whole is constructed and passed over to the production side of the airline. It is essential that a single channel be established for this purpose, if the marketing department is to function comprehensively within its terms of reference. If this is not done, those responsible for production will start by being confused through receiving conflicting commercial requirements, and will finish by deciding between them, which means they will be making decisions.

All these processes are, in a sense, preparatory, in that they are designed to plan the product which has the best chance of being marketed at a profit, taking into account the external controls exercised on airline operation, and the revenue to be expected from its sale.

The next series of stages are the active operational marketing functions.

7 The final schedules now having been settled, the customers have to be attracted to the point of sale by advertising and sales promotion techniques, and by personal canvassing of traffic.

8 At the point of sale, salesmanship has to be used to clinch the sale.

9 To ensure sales, all sales points have to be provided with rapid and efficient access to the capacity which is available.

As set out in these terms, one sees the marketing department in its tactical working. Within the framework of a given set of resources and an established regulatory pattern, the task is to optimise the results of the analysis and subsequent attack on the market. This almost certainly means achievement of the most satisfactory balance between expenditure and revenue that is attainable. The latter consideration may be tempered somewhat by longer term considerations. For example, a service may be deliberately offered in the short term at a loss because forecasts demonstrate that this particular part of the product will, at some acceptable time in the future, move into a profit-making situation. On the whole, however, seasonal planning and selling are aimed at getting the best financial return possible, consistent with sound operations, within a given set of circumstances.

Concurrently with this short term planning and activity, longer term, strategic work has to go on in the marketing side, and most functions will be concerned in this, some very much more than others. Although within each Branch there may be short and long term specialists, it will almost certainly make for the most efficient coordination between the immediate and longer term plans, if the men concerned with each aspect are both controlled functionally within a Branch or Section which is bi-focal in this respect.

Going back over the processes which have already been examined in their tactical aspects, each can be seen to have a parallel strategic part to play.

1 Market Research. Long term forecasts will be necessary in order that (in particular) aircraft provisioning, aircrew recruitment and training, traffic handling, building and capital availability—all of which require long notice—can be organised to meet traffic as it arises years ahead.

2 Fares and Rates. IATA agreements are now generally concluded on a two year basis, with provision for short term variations of particular promotional tariffs to meet changes in the marketing situation. In any case, long term plans can only sensibly be made against forecasts of expenditure and revenue. The market research traffic forecasts must be allied with *price* forecasts before a projection of revenue is possible.

3 Those responsible for ensuring that traffic rights and licences are available for the services that the airline operates, must be supplied with long term forecasts of likely developments (new routes etc.), as achievement of any extensions to a network usually requires long and complex negotiation.

K

4 Co-ordination of requirements. In the same way that the short term requirement has to be fed into the operating machinery, so must the results of long term commercial thinking (for example, size and competitive qualities of future aircraft, changes in distribution of traffic by class of travel as well as over-all changes in traffic revenue), so that the assets of the future are planned qualitatively as well as quantitatively.

5 Relations with other airlines. Particularly where co-operative arrangements are in force, the long term forecasting of the airline must be matched with the similar plans emerging from other airlines operating in parallel.

6 Promotion. This rarely plans as far ahead as the other functions. Even so, those responsible for promotion, whilst concentrating very largely on the present and the immediate future, must be thinking well ahead if their programmes are to fit changing social and expenditure habits, among other things. For example, census forecasts which demonstrate a shift in the age distribution of the population are used to formulate the necessary variations in advertising emphasis and media selection, in readiness for the changed market of the future.

7 Point of Sale. The future requirement cannot be met by hurried short term opening or closing of points of sale as demand changes in quantity or geographical distribution. As in all other cases, the basic forecast of traffic that will be offering must be used to ensure that none is lost through an inadequate network, nor that sales are spread too thinly over far too many airline offices and agencies.

8 Reservations. Almost more than any other marketing function, this needs to plan its future facilities so that rising pressure is always efficiently accommodated. The quickest way to lose traffic that is on offer is to have a reservation system which is inadequate, for immediately *all* bookings become frustrated, not just those marginal additions that have caused the problem.

Stepping back and looking at this somewhat detailed picture critically, the airline in its organisation has to ensure that *all* functions are not only fully covered as vertical divisions within the complete marketing block, but that there is also a horizontal stratification through all the processes of:

(*a*) Policy formulation, influencing and influenced by, the facts of:
  (i) long term planning;
  (ii) short term planning.

(*b*) Issue of directives resulting from policies and plans;

(*c*) Day to day operation by the field force of the marketing functions *vis à vis* the customers, in accordance with policy directives;

(*d*) Assessment of the results.

It is apparent that (*a*), (*b*) and (*d*) are Head Office functions, and that the field activities embraced in (*c*) are separate. What is not obvious is how the Head Office functions should relate to each other and how the field should relate (organisationally) to Head Office.

At this point it is necessary to look at the complete airline organisation and formulate some views. The writer believes that the pattern which recognises two line functions, marketing and production (or operations), separating immediately below the Chief Executive, with staff functions (finance and personnel primarily, but there may be others) also reporting to him, is fundamentally the one that is potentially the most efficient. The whole purpose of management is to make decisions, and the object of an organisation is to enable all echelons of management to make the best decisions of which they are capable, everybody knowing clearly which decisions are his and the channels whereby his knowledge can be fed up and/or across the organisation, to assist decision-making by others.

If the two-pronged marketing/operations division is blurred or fragmented, disembodied planning tends to materialise to fill the decision-making gaps that appear.

Plans are the servants of action, and neither the marketing department nor the operations department can be held finally responsible for their activities if they work to plans emanating from amorphous bodies external to their own authority. Of course, it is possible to argue cogently that, since all plans must be agreed by the Chief Executive, who carries the final responsibility, he needs his own planning staff to aid his judgment of the plans of the line departments. But this is not inconsistent with handing full responsibility to the line departments for both planning and execution, for the function of the Chief Executive's staff is basically analytical and advisory.

There can be no compromise between:

(*a*) The concept of a fully responsible *marketing* department, constantly working with the production side to plan the most saleable schedules consistent with economical production, assessing the revenue that will emerge (and defending this to the Chief Executive) and then being judged on its success in getting the money in;
and
(*b*) A *sales* department with a given product and given sales targets.

However much, in the latter case, the sales department's views are sought, the scales will now be tipped towards 'selling what can be produced' and the area of excuses for non-performance will be enlarged.

There are personal and inter-departmental tensions in every major business. The 'fully responsible' concept of marketing is much less productive of these tensions than the 'central planning' concept.

In devising an organisational structure it is useful to remember that the slots will be filled by people, and a system that relies on too many checks and balances, to insure against mistakes, will end up by insuring against decisions too, because eventually no one will feel he has complete functional responsibility.

So far as the marketing side is concerned, therefore, the various functions at Head Office need to be grouped in such a way that the senior marketing executive is responsible for formulating policy *and* constructing long and short term plans. All these will need to be cleared as to practicability and cost with the operating side, of course. But there should be nobody in the airline except the Chief Executive to criticise the policy and plans from the purely marketing point of view. Since marketing, unlike, say, engineering or accountancy, is an occupation not requiring qualifications, others in the airline will frequently be vocal on the concomitants of marketing, particularly advertising. But this is a small cross that all marketing men have to bear, and the fact that they often have to defend their actions un-officially to their colleagues is probably useful rather than the op-posite, so long as full responsibility lies with them.

The instrument of marketing policy and plans is the field organi-sation. So it follows that establishments and budgets in the field must be those which the Head Office marketing department regard as adequate for the task. It also follows that control and check of the field force by means of achievement targets must also be the responsi-bility of the same department.

Any widespread organisation will always suffer from some degree of mistrust between Head Office and the field. To the field, Head Office is bureaucratic, inflexible, uncomprehending. To Head Office, men in the field are irresponsible, limited of vision, and always going about things in the wrong way instead of following the tidy pro-cedures laid down for them. And within limits both points of view are right.

Although emotional problems between Head Office and the field can never be completely eliminated, so far as the marketing side is concerned a good deal of friction will be avoided if the field managers:

(*a*) Are consulted on all aspects of the short term product, but parti-cularly as regards timing of services;

(*b*) Put their establishments up for approval, these being treated in a way that is seen to be reasonable and just over time;

(*c*) Are consulted on targets;

(*d*) Are given policy guidance on method, help when required, and then left to get on with the job without interference, subject to ade-quate performance.

INDEX